play guitar with...

the smiths

Compiled by Nick Crispin
Music arranged by Arthur Dick
Music processed by Paul Ewers Music Design
Cover designed by Fresh Lemon
Cover photograph courtesy of Stephen Wright / smithphotos.com

To access companion recorded demonstration
and backing tracks online, visit:
www.halleonard.com/mylibrary

7113-4895-8369-0952

Audio recorded, mixed and mastered by Jonas Persson & John Rose
All guitars by Arthur Dick
Bass by Paul Townsend
Drums by Brett Morgan

Order No. AM983180
ISBN 978-1-84609-117-9

Visit Hal Leonard Online at
www.halleonard.com

World headquarters, contact:
Hal Leonard
7777 West Bluemound Road
Milwaukee, WI 53213
Email: info@halleonard.com

In Europe, contact:
Hal Leonard Europe Limited
1 Red Place
London, W1K 6PL
Email: info@halleonardeurope.com

In Australia, contact:
Hal Leonard Australia Pty. Ltd.
4 Lentara Court
Cheltenham, Victoria, 3192 Australia
Email: info@halleonard.com.au

guitar tablature explained

guitar notation can be notated in three different ways: on a musical stave, in tablature, and in rhythm slashes

RHYTHM SLASHES are written above the stave. Strum chords in the rhythm indicated. Round noteheads indicate single notes.

THE MUSICAL STAVE shows pitches and rhythms and is divided by lines into bars. Pitches are named after the first seven letters of the alphabet.

TABLATURE graphically represents the guitar fingerboard. Each horizontal line represents a string, and each number represents a fret.

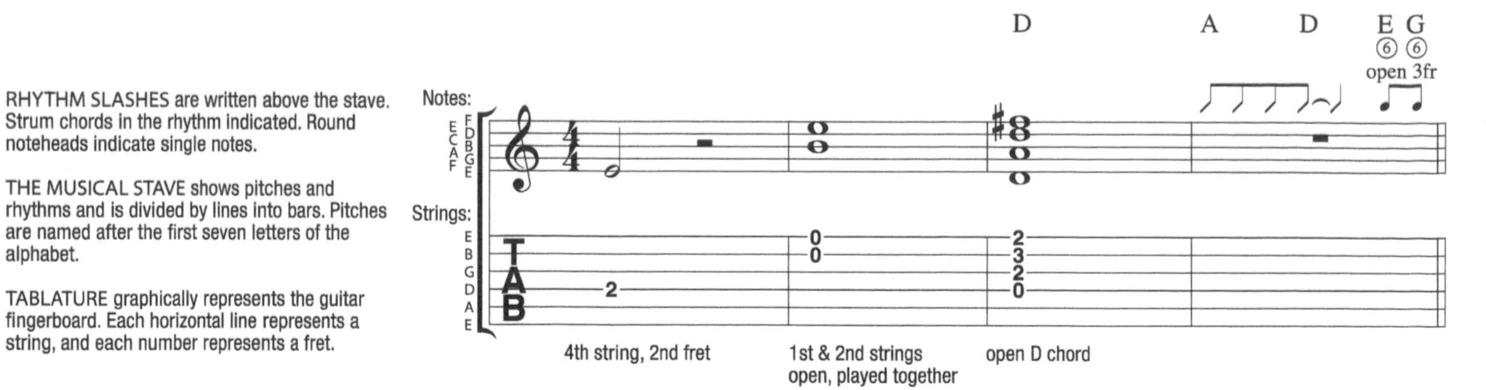

definitions for special guitar notation

SEMI-TONE BEND: Strike the note and bend up a semi-tone (1/2 step).

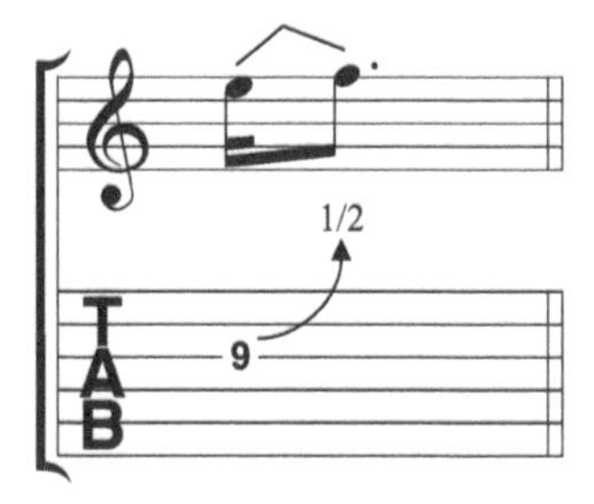

WHOLE-TONE BEND: Strike the note and bend up a whole-tone (whole step).

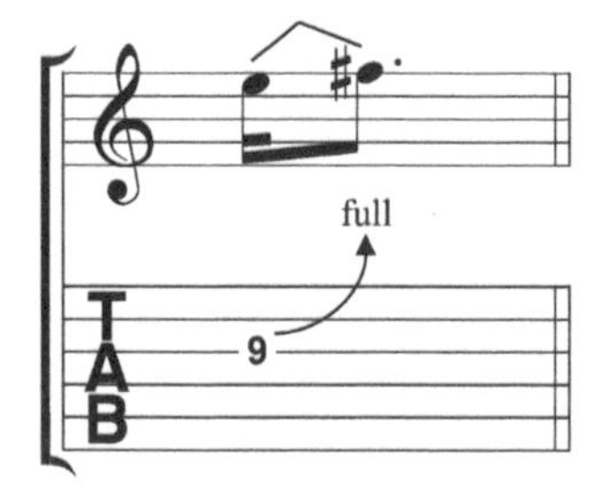

GRACE NOTE BEND: Strike the note and bend as indicated. Play the first note as quickly as possible.

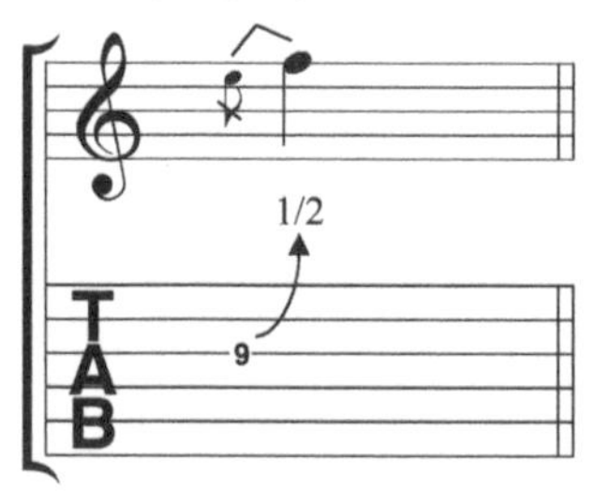

QUARTER-TONE BEND: Strike the note and bend up a 1/4 step.

BEND & RELEASE: Strike the note and bend up as indicated, then release back to the original note.

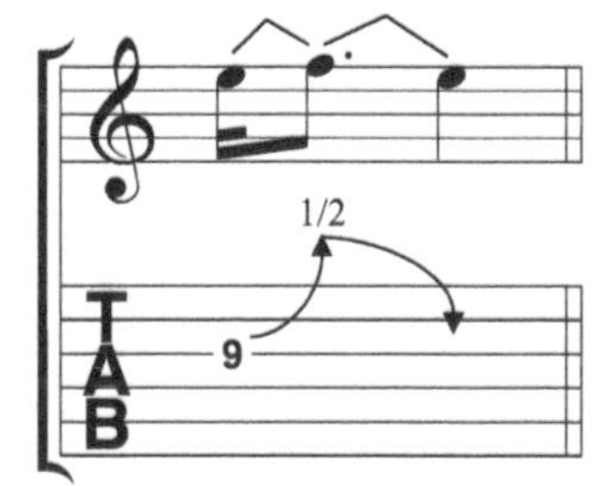

COMPOUND BEND & RELEASE: Strike the note and bend up and down in the rhythm indicated.

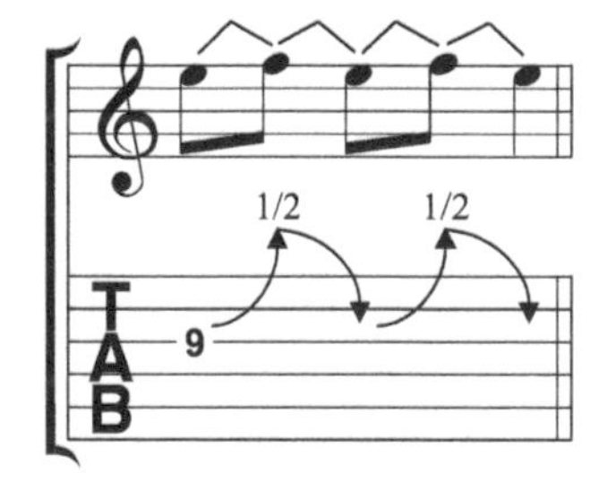

PRE-BEND: Bend the note as indicated, then strike it.

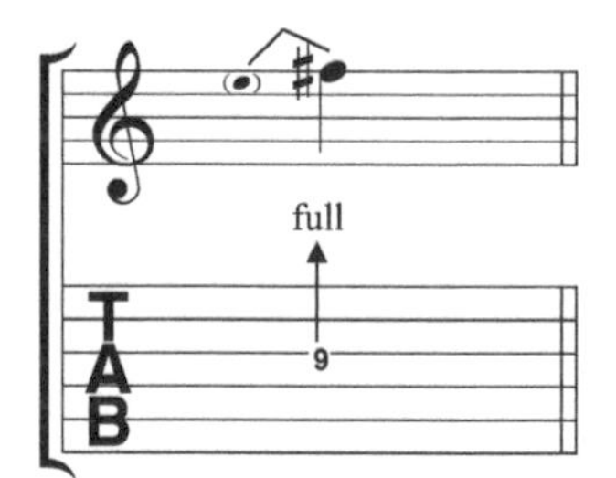

PRE-BEND & RELEASE: Bend the note as indicated. Strike it and release the note back to the original pitch.

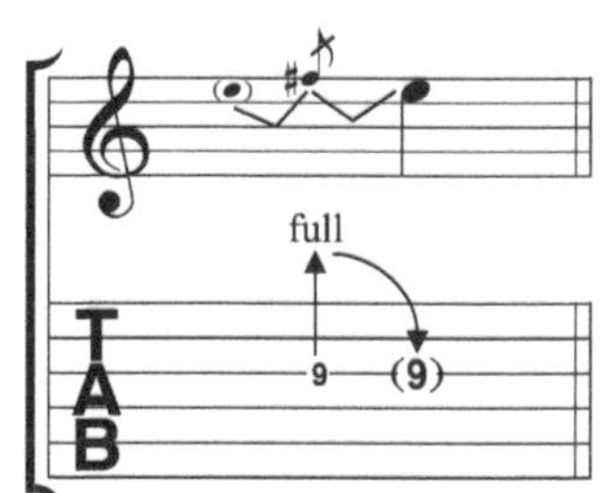

HAMMER-ON: Strike the first note with one finger, then sound the second note (on the same string) with another finger by fretting it without picking.

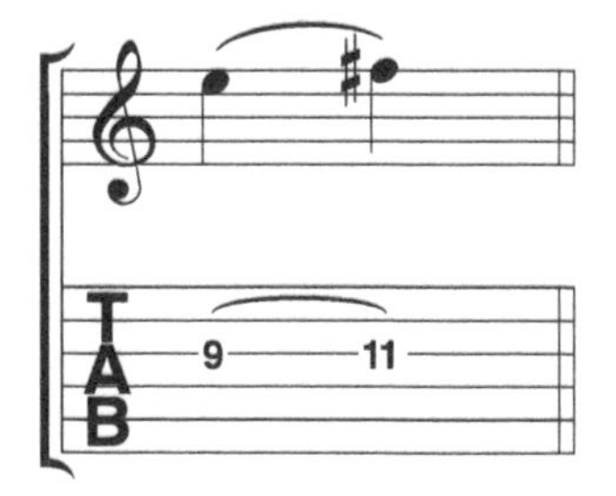

PULL-OFF: Place both fingers on the notes to be sounded, strike the first note and without picking, pull the finger off to sound the second note.

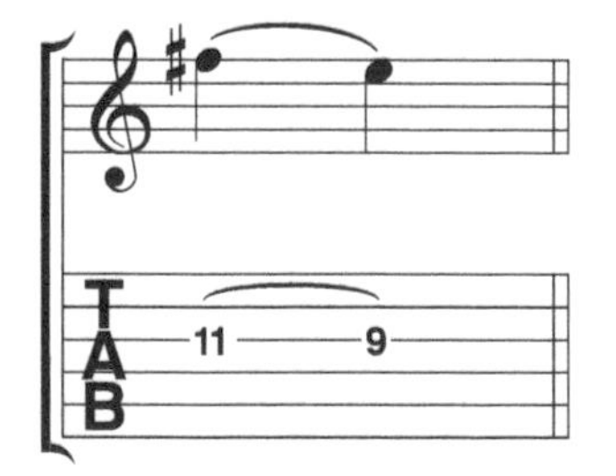

LEGATO SLIDE (GLISS): Strike the first note and then slide the same fret-hand finger up or down to the second note. The second note is not struck.

MUFFLED STRINGS: A percussive sound is produced by laying the fret hand across the string(s) without depressing, and striking them with the pick hand.

NATURAL HARMONIC: Strike the note while the fret-hand lightly touches the string directly over the fret indicated.

PICK SCRAPE: The edge of the pick is rubbed down (or up) the string, producing a scratchy sound.

PALM MUTING: The note is partially muted by the pick hand lightly touching the string(s) just before the bridge.

SHIFT SLIDE (GLISS & RESTRIKE): Same as legato slide, except the second note is struck.

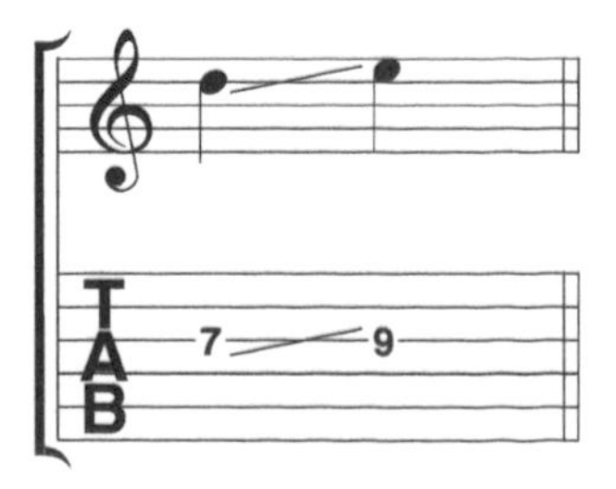

NOTE: The speed of any bend is indicated by the music notation and tempo.

SHIFT SLIDE (GLISS & RESTRIKE): Same as legato slide, except the second note is struck.

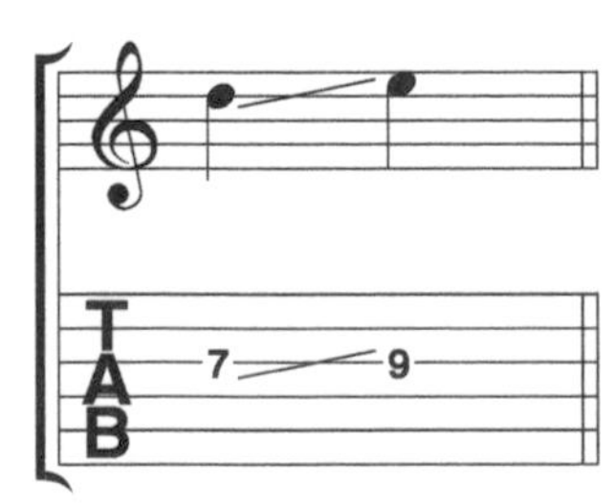

TRILL: Very rapidly alternate between the notes indicated by continuously hammering on and pulling off.

TAPPING: Hammer ("tap") the fret indicated with the pick-hand index or middle finger and pull off to the note fretted by the fret hand.

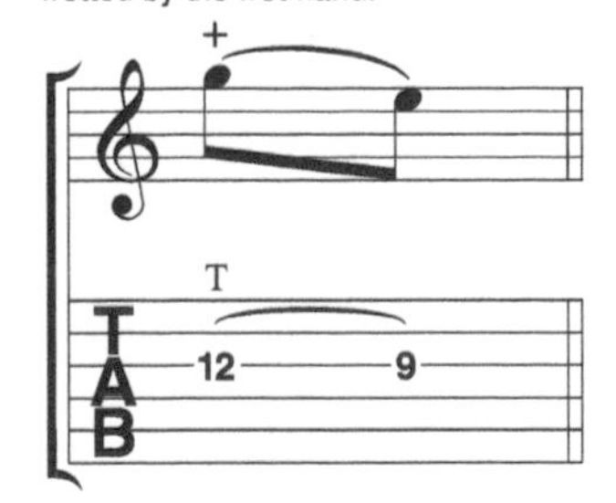

PICK SCRAPE: The edge of the pick is rubbed down (or up) the string, producing a scratchy sound.

MUFFLED STRINGS: A percussive sound is produced by laying the fret hand across the string(s) without depressing, and striking them with the pick hand.

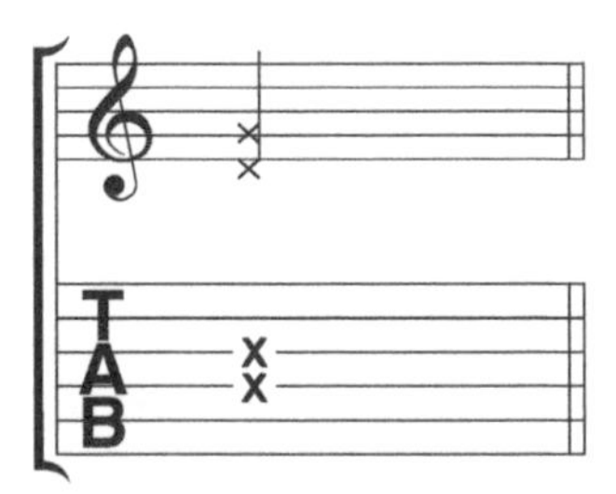

NATURAL HARMONIC: Strike the note while the fret-hand lightly touches the string directly over the fret indicated.

PINCH HARMONIC: The note is fretted normally and a harmonic is produced by adding the edge of the thumb or the tip of the index finger of the pick hand to the normal pick attack.

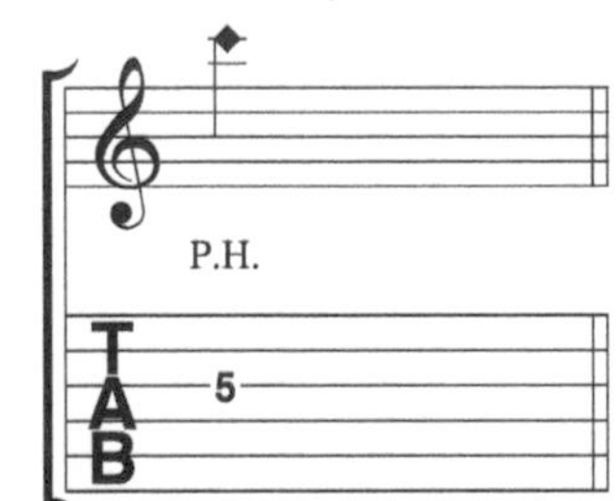

HARP HARMONIC: The note is fretted normally and a harmonic is produced by gently resting the pick hand's index finger directly above the indicated fret (in brackets) while plucking the appropriate string.

PALM MUTING: The note is partially muted by the pick hand lightly touching the string(s) just before the bridge.

RAKE: Drag the pick across the strings indicated with a single motion.

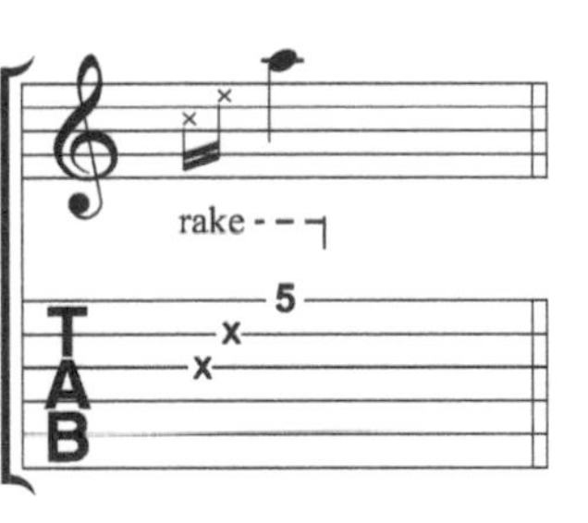

TREMOLO PICKING: The note is picked as rapidly and continuously as possible.

ARPEGGIATE: Play the notes of the chord indicated by quickly rolling them from bottom to top.

SWEEP PICKING: Rhythmic downstroke and/or upstroke motion across the strings.

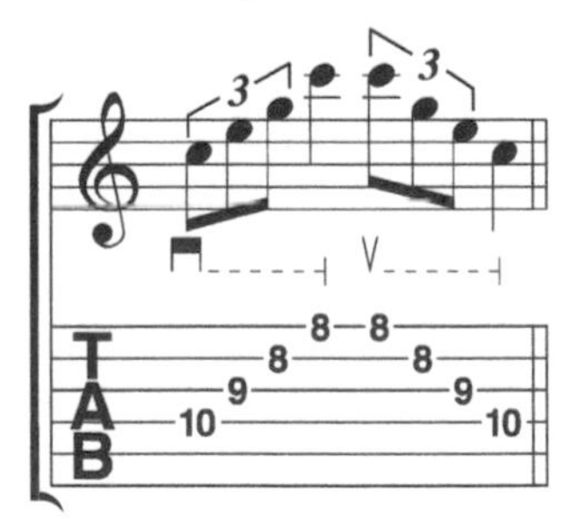

VIBRATO DIVE BAR AND RETURN: The pitch of the note or chord is dropped a specific number of steps (in rhythm) then returned to the original pitch.

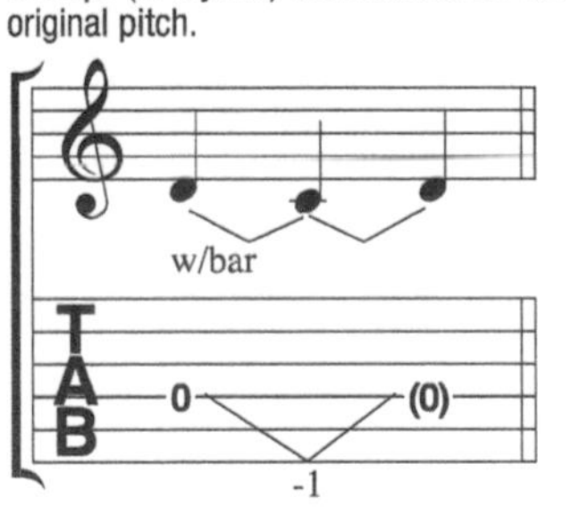

VIBRATO BAR SCOOP: Depress the bar just before striking the note, then quickly release the bar.

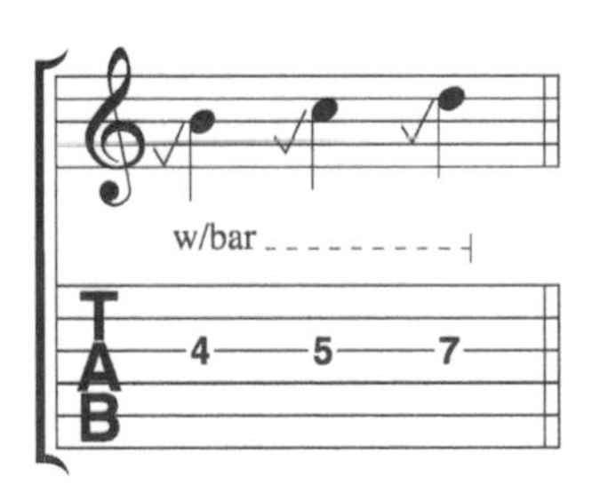

VIBRATO BAR DIP: Strike the note and then immediately drop a specific number of steps, then release back to the original pitch.

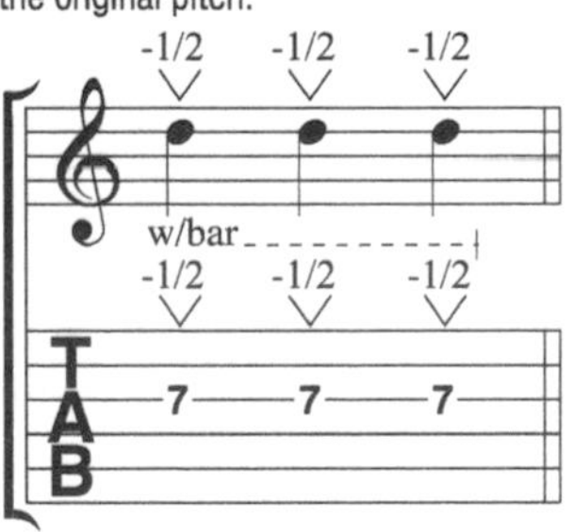

additional musical definitions

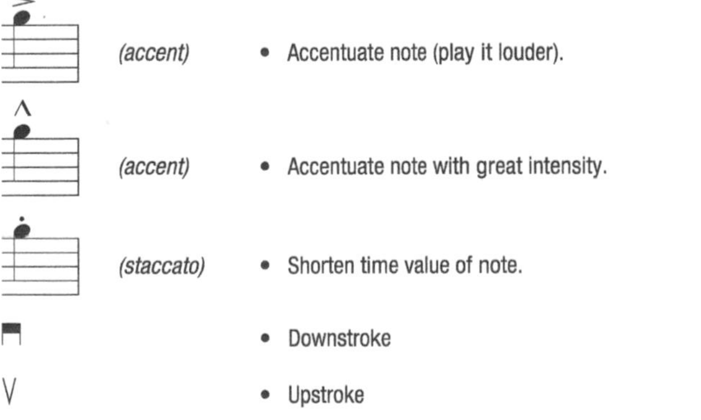

	(accent)	• Accentuate note (play it louder).
	(accent)	• Accentuate note with great intensity.
	(staccato)	• Shorten time value of note.
		• Downstroke
		• Upstroke

NOTE: Tablature numbers in brackets mean:
1. The note is sustained, but a new articulation (such as hammer on or slide) begins.
2. A note may be fretted but not necessarily played.

D.%. al Coda	• Go back to the sign (%), then play until the bar marked ***To Coda*** ⊕ then skip to the section marked ⊕ ***Coda***.
D.C. al Fine	• Go back to the beginning of the song and play until the bar marked ***Fine***.
tacet	• Instrument is silent (drops out).
	• Repeat bars between signs.

• When a repeated section has different endings, play the first ending only the first time and the second ending only the second time.

bigmouth strikes again

Words & Music by Morrissey & Johnny Marr

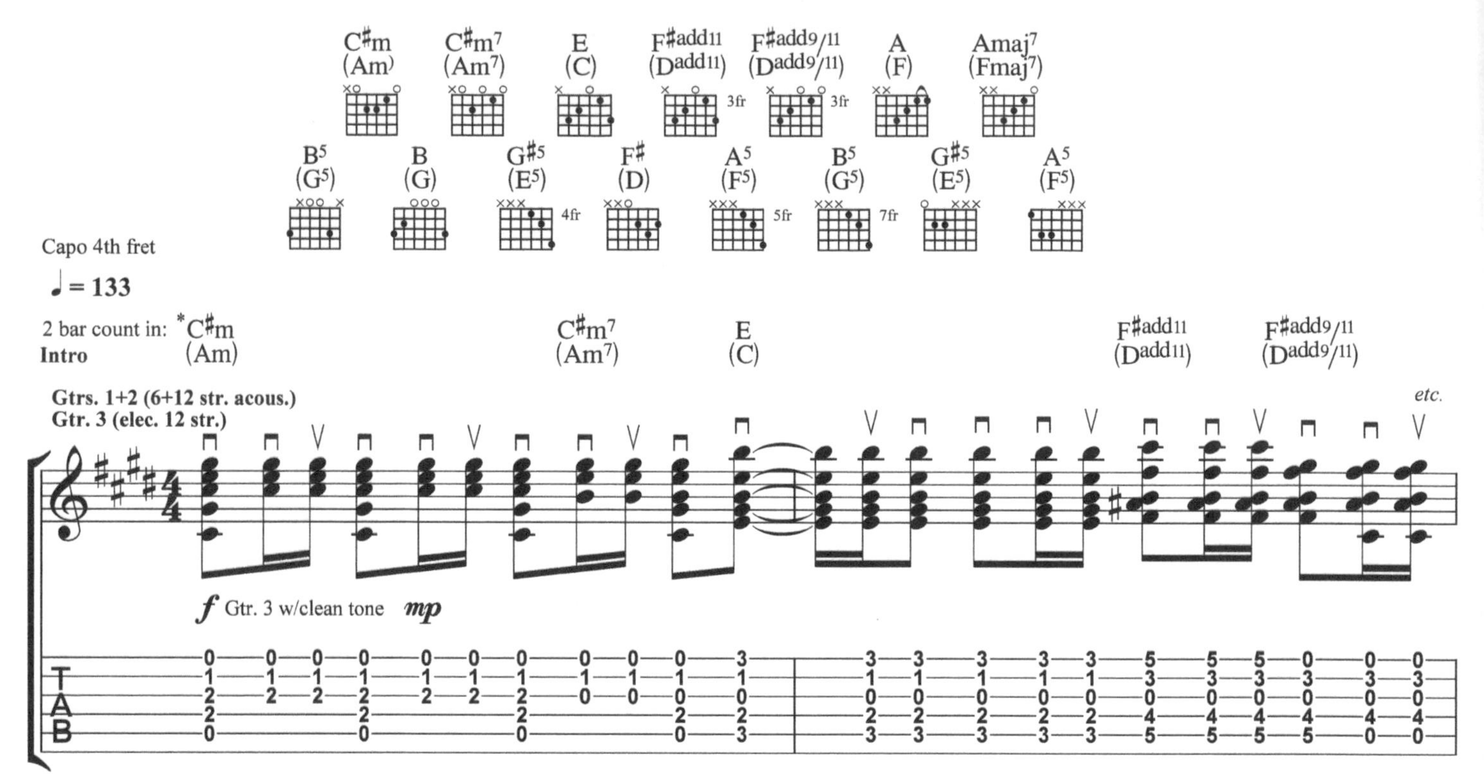

* Symbols in parenthesis represent chord names with respect to capoed guitar. (Tab 0 = 4th fret)
Symbols above represent actual sounding chords.

Play written part (elec.) throughout

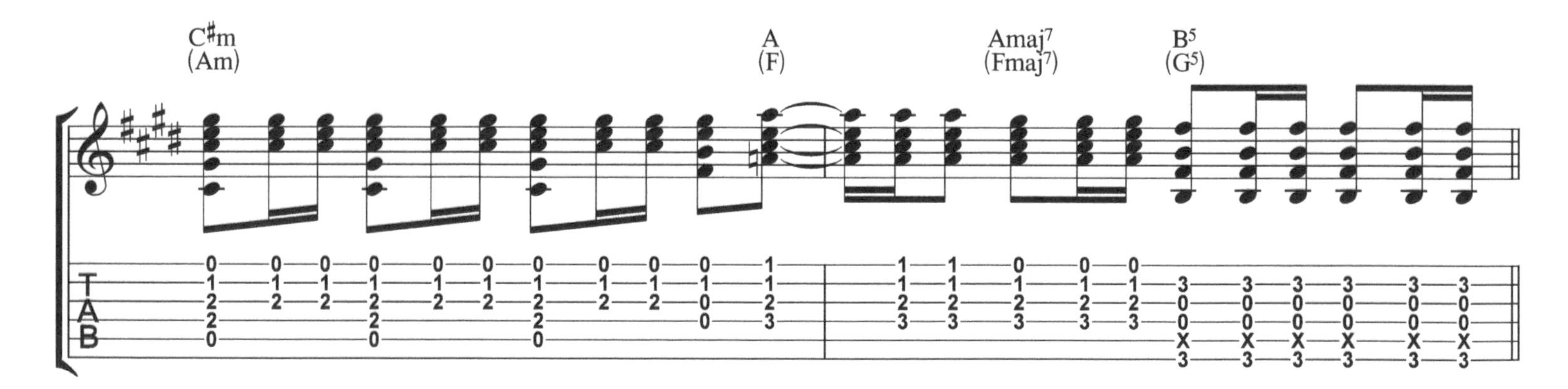

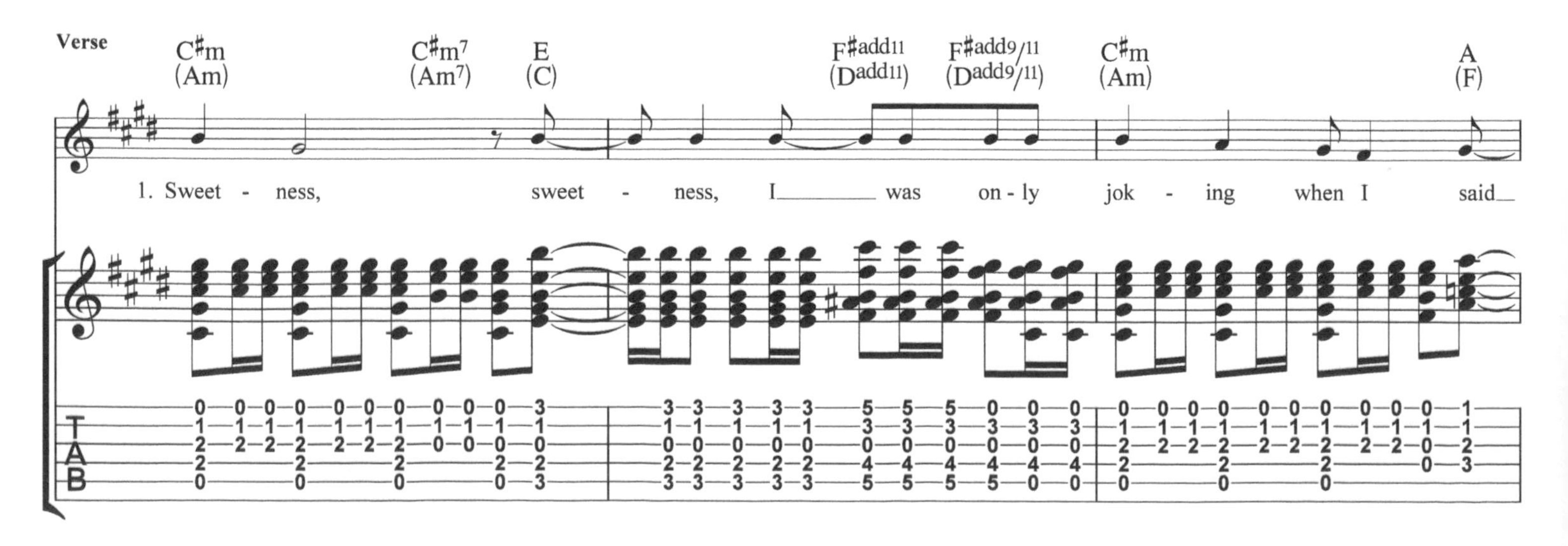

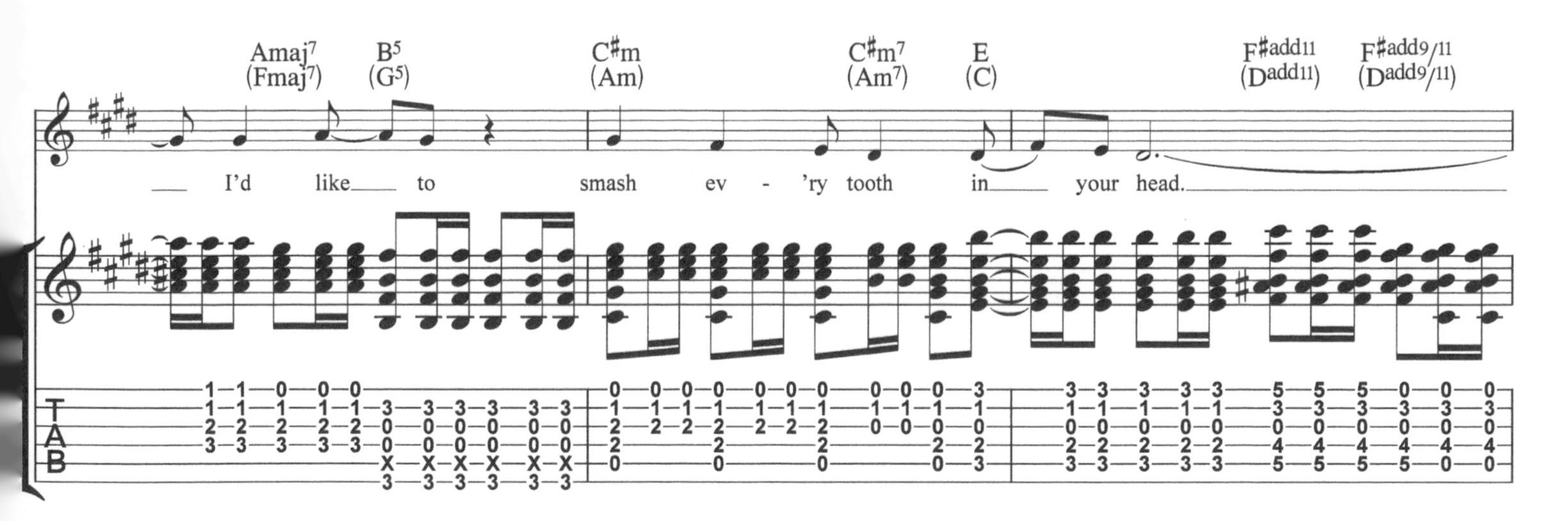
Amaj7 (Fmaj7) B5 (G5) C♯m (Am) C♯m7 (Am7) E (C) F♯add11 (Dadd11) F♯add9/11 (Dadd9/11)
I'd like to smash ev - 'ry tooth in your head.
TAB

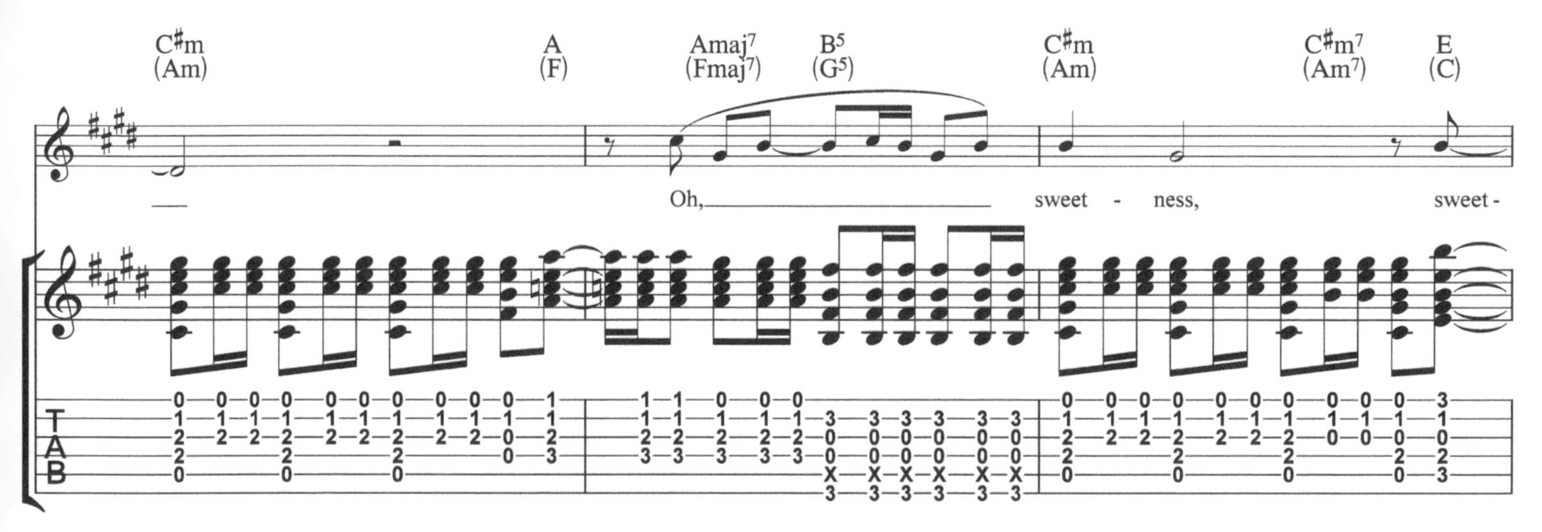
C♯m (Am) A (F) Amaj7 (Fmaj7) B5 (G5) C♯m (Am) C♯m7 (Am7) E (C)
Oh, sweet - ness, sweet -
TAB

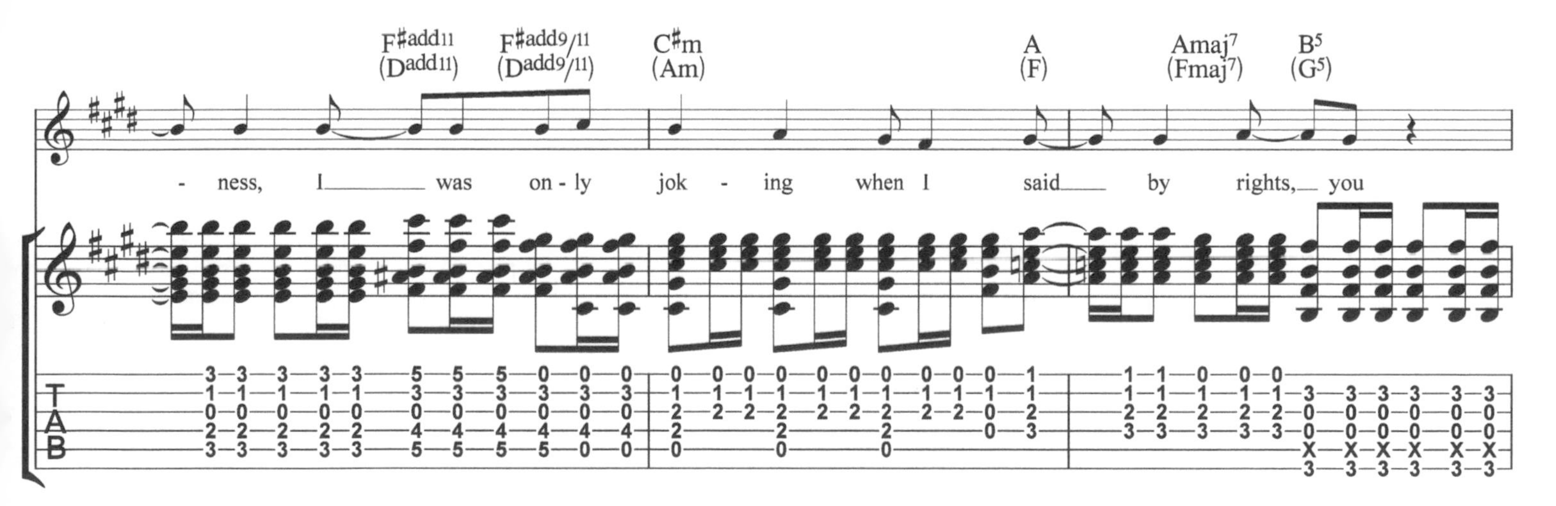
F♯add11 (Dadd11) F♯add9/11 (Dadd9/11) C♯m (Am) A (F) Amaj7 (Fmaj7) B5 (G5)
- ness, I was on - ly jok - ing when I said by rights, you
TAB

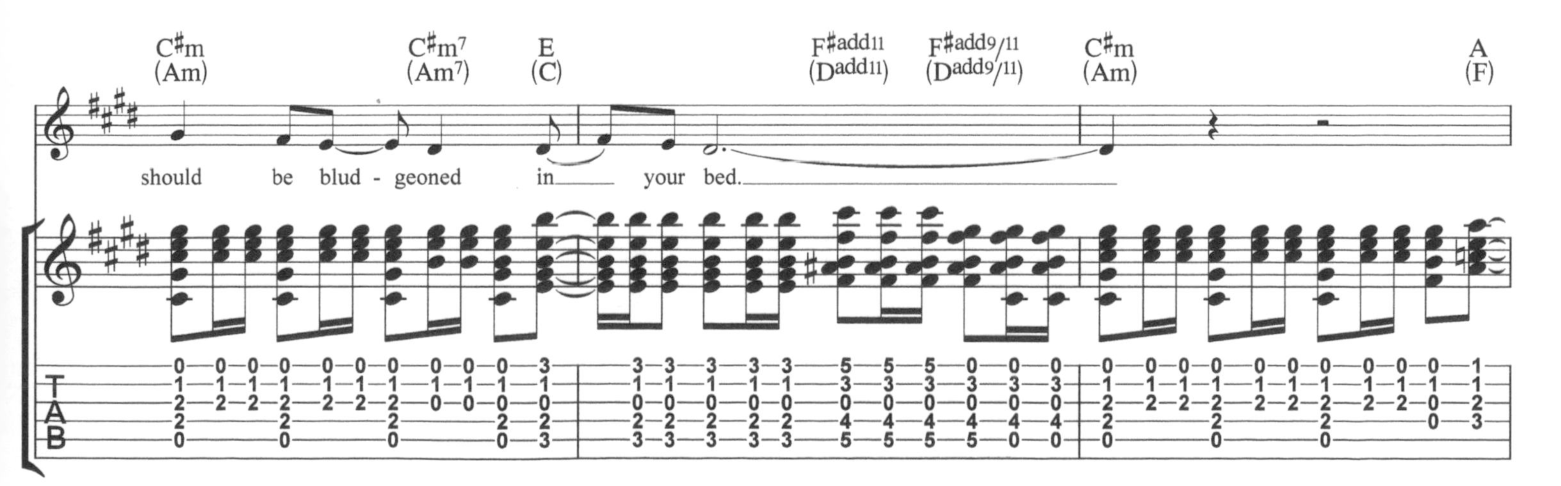
C♯m (Am) C♯m7 (Am7) E (C) F♯add11 (Dadd11) F♯add9/11 (Dadd9/11) C♯m (Am) A (F)
should be blud - geoned in your bed.
TAB

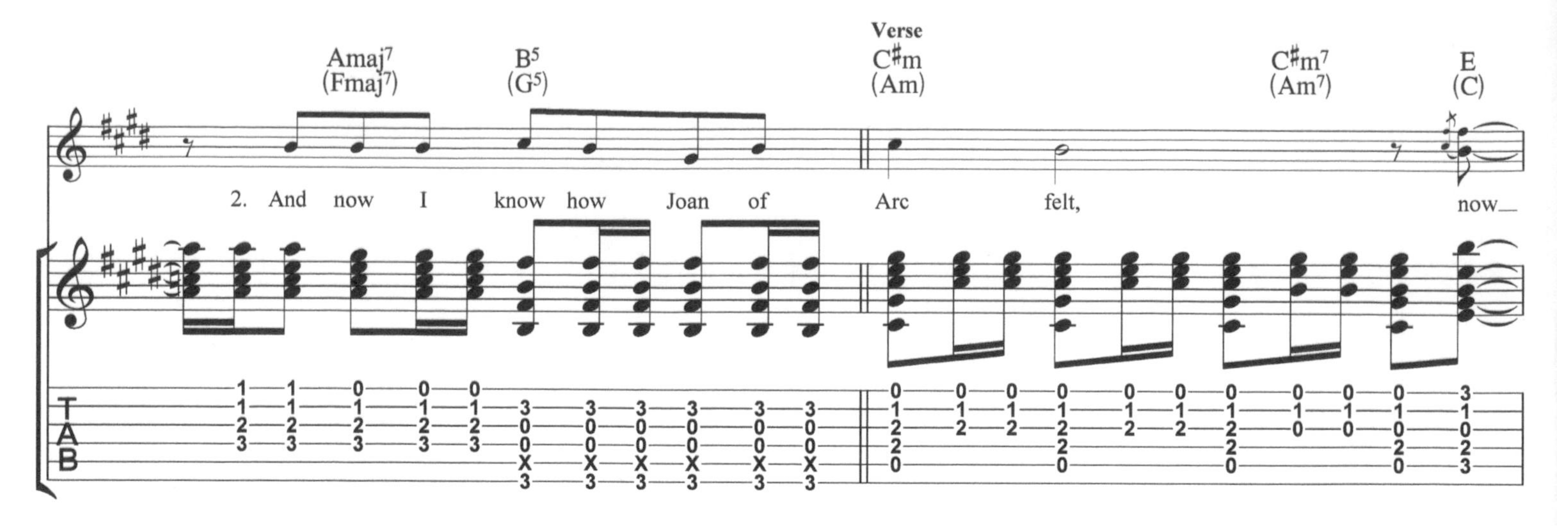
Verse
Amaj7 (Fmaj7)
B5 (G5)
C♯m (Am)
C♯m7 (Am7)
E (C)
2. And now I know how Joan of Arc felt, now

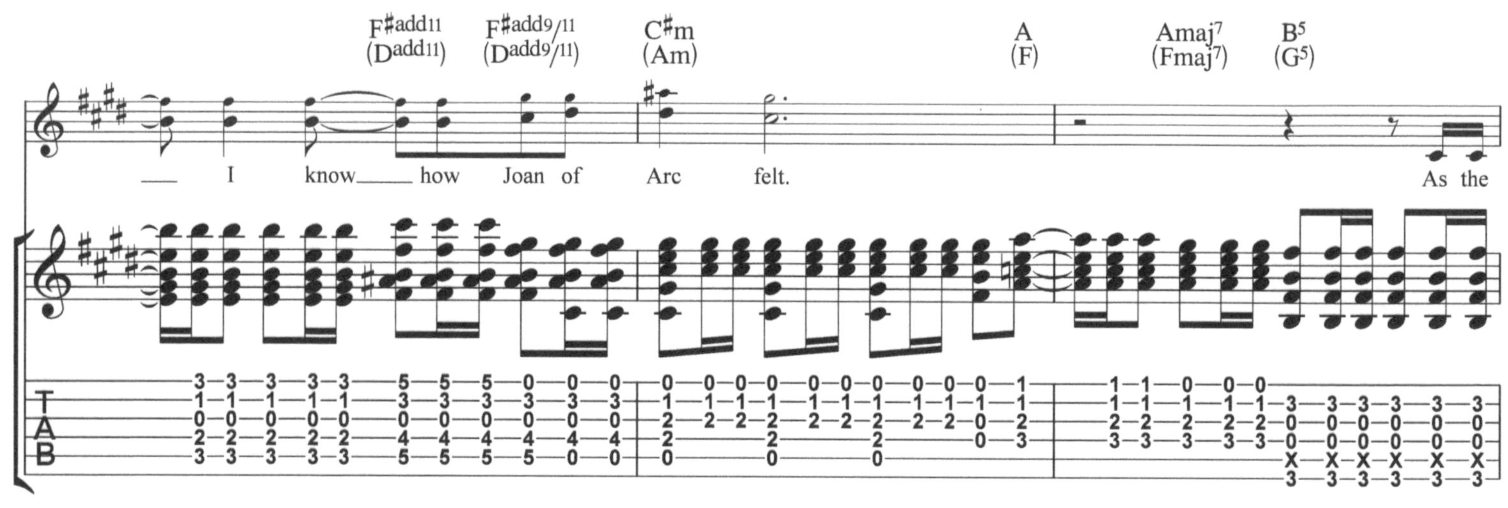
F♯add11 (Dadd11)
F♯add9/11 (Dadd9/11)
C♯m (Am)
A (F)
Amaj7 (Fmaj7)
B5 (G5)
I know how Joan of Arc felt. As the

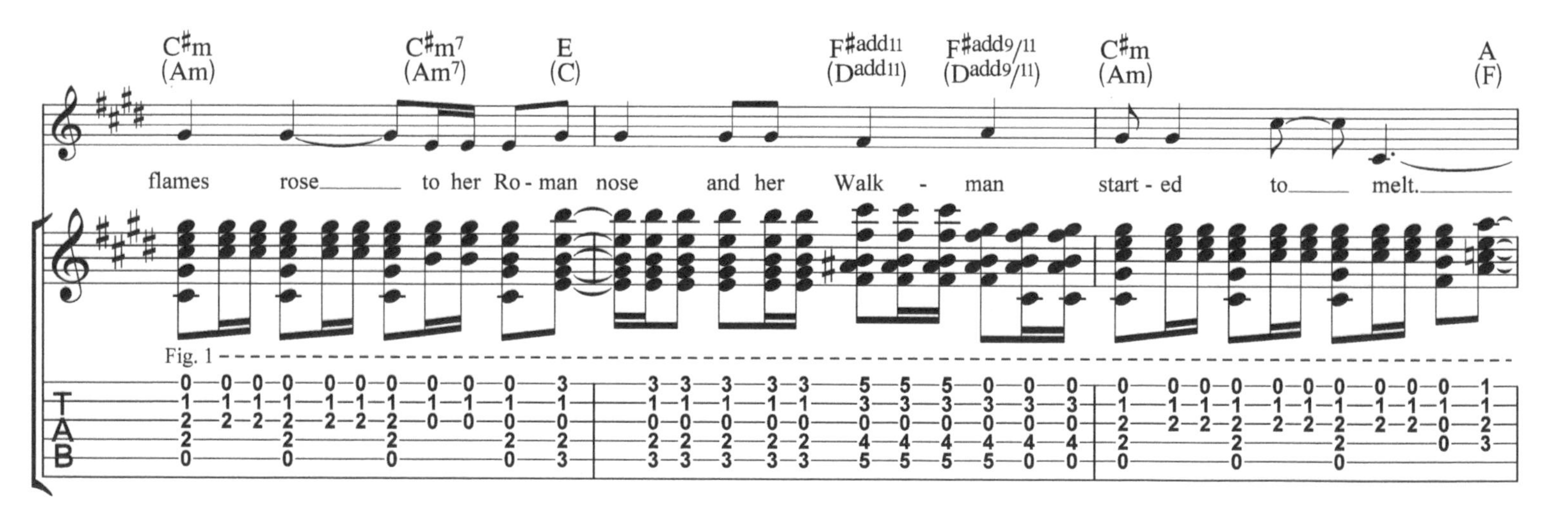
C♯m (Am)
C♯m7 (Am7)
E (C)
F♯add11 (Dadd11)
F♯add9/11 (Dadd9/11)
C♯m (Am)
A (F)
flames rose to her Ro-man nose and her Walk - man start - ed to melt.
Fig. 1

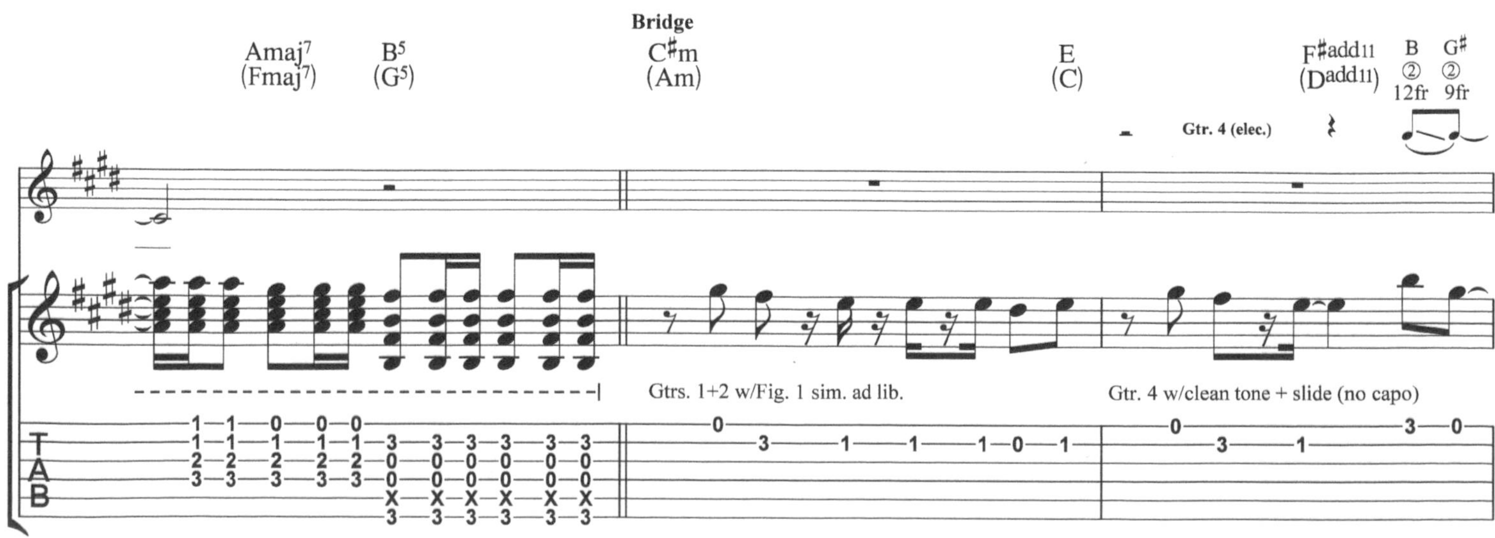
Bridge
Amaj7 (Fmaj7)
B5 (G5)
C♯m (Am)
E (C)
F♯add11 (Dadd11)
B ② 12fr
G♯ ② 9fr
Gtr. 4 (elec.)
Gtrs. 1+2 w/Fig. 1 sim. ad lib.
Gtr. 4 w/clean tone + slide (no capo)

C♯m
(Am)
A
(F)
B5
(G5)
C♯m
(Am)
E
(C)
F♯add11
(Dadd11)
B
②
12fr
G♯
②
9fr
Ooh,
ooh.

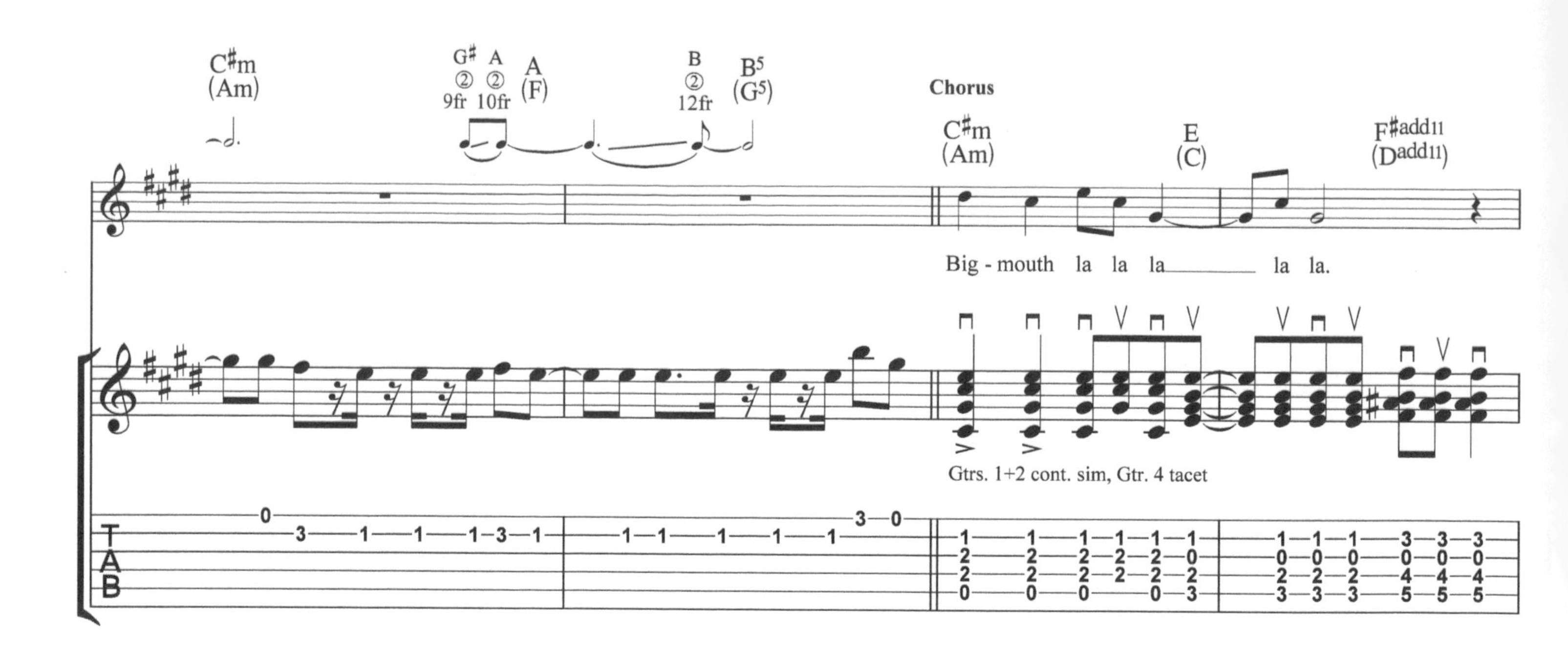
C#m (Am)
G# A 9fr 10fr
A (F)
B 12fr
B5 (G5)
Chorus
C#m (Am)
E (C)
F#add11 (Dadd11)
Big - mouth la la la la la.
Gtrs. 1+2 cont. sim, Gtr. 4 tacet

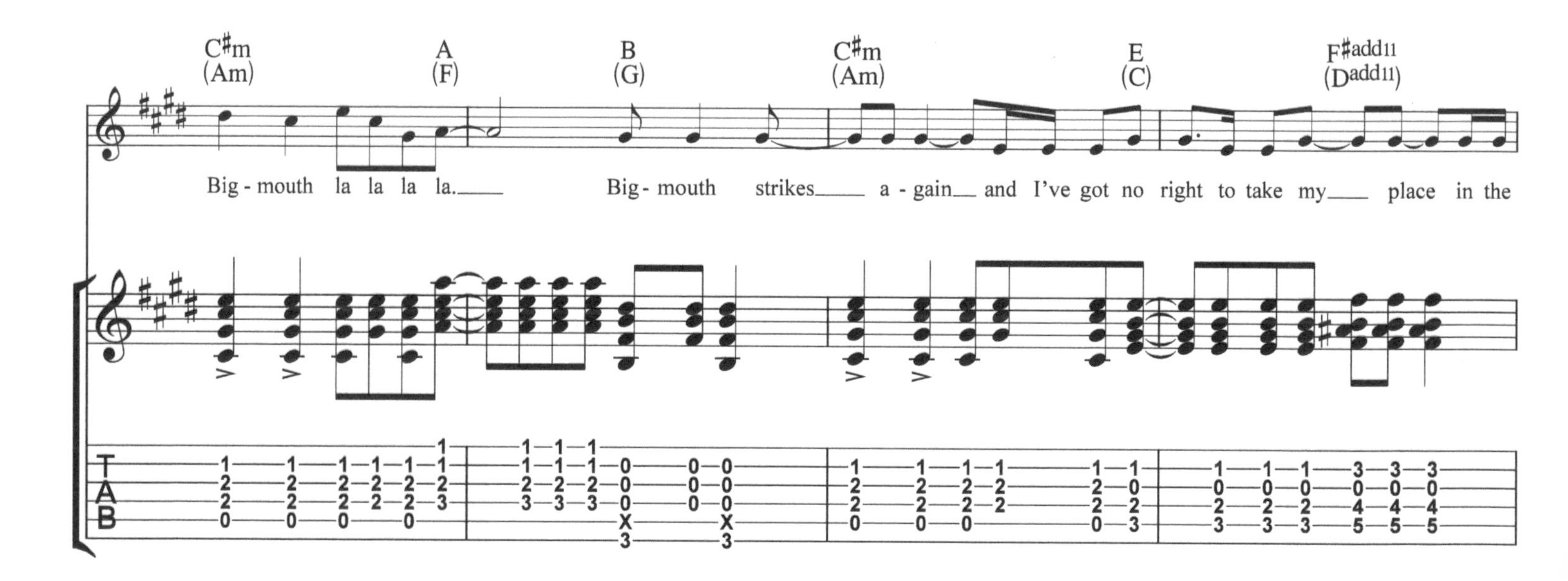
C#m (Am)
A (F)
B (G)
C#m (Am)
E (C)
F#add11 (Dadd11)
Big - mouth la la la la. Big - mouth strikes a - gain and I've got no right to take my place in the

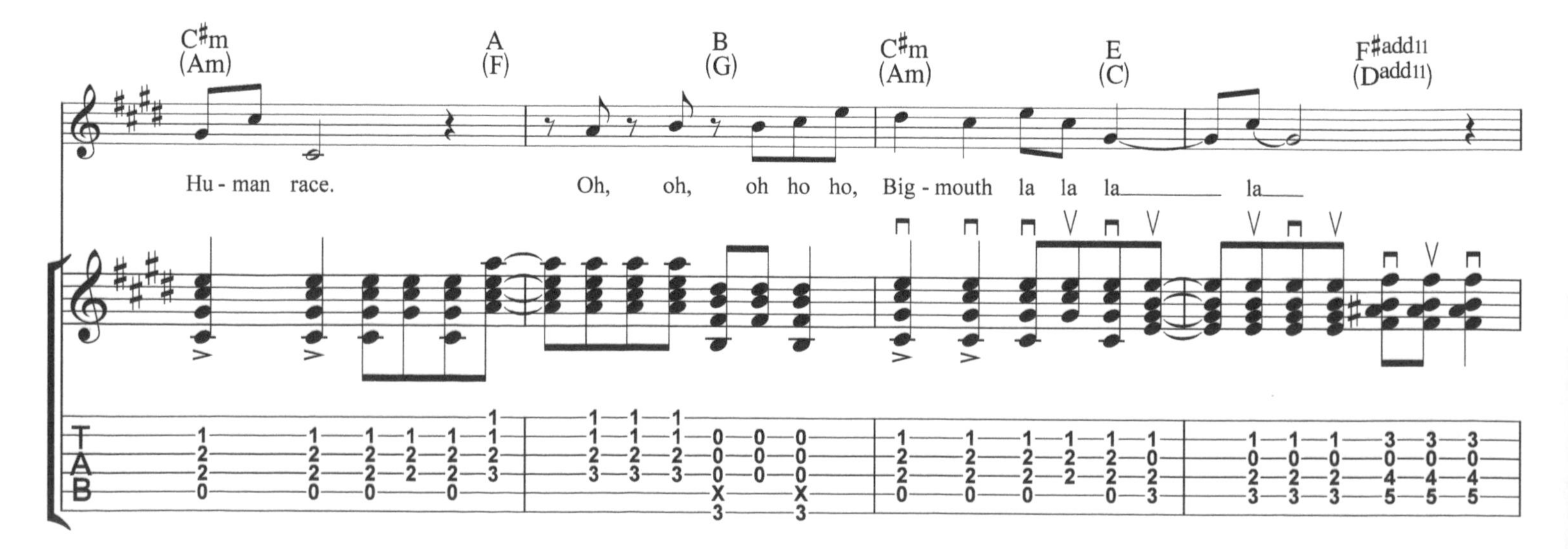
C#m (Am)
A (F)
B (G)
C#m (Am)
E (C)
F#add11 (Dadd11)
Hu - man race. Oh, oh, oh ho ho, Big - mouth la la la la

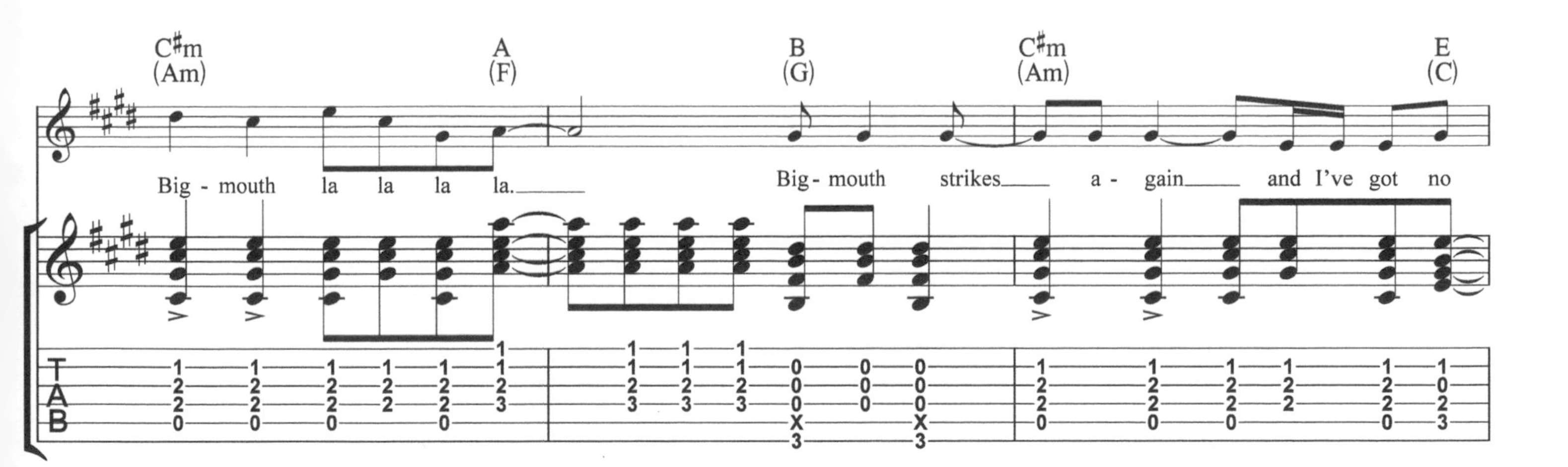
C♯m
(Am)
A
(F)
B
(G)
C♯m
(Am)
E
(C)
Big - mouth la la la la.
Big - mouth strikes a - gain and I've got no
T
A
B

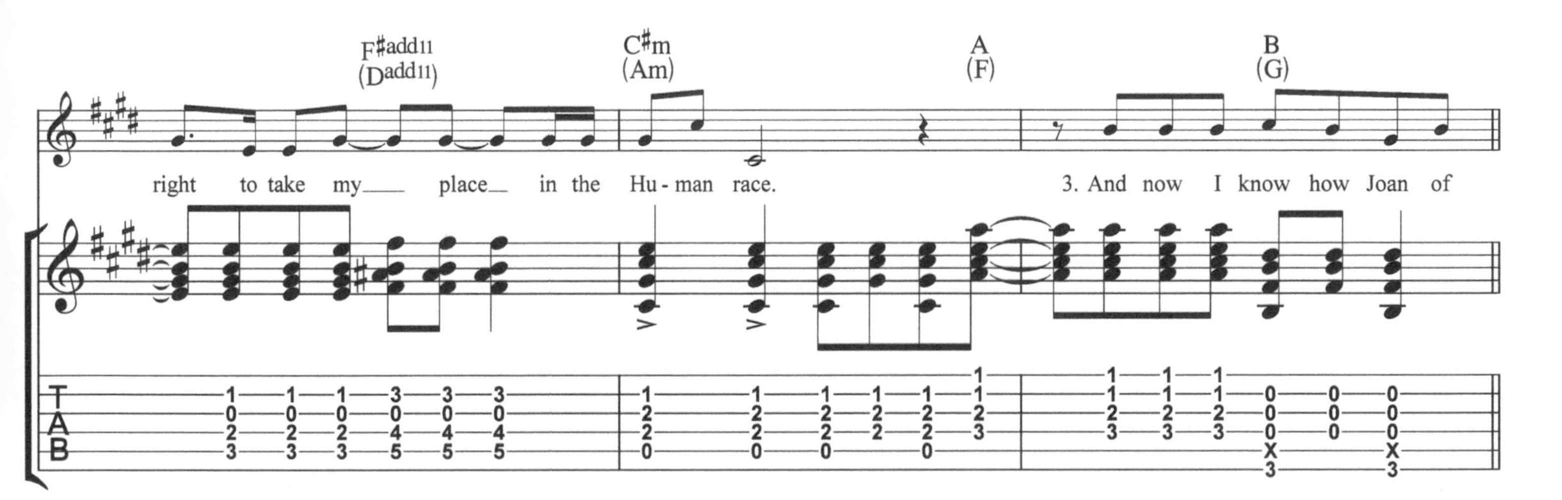
F♯add11
(Dadd11)
C♯m
(Am)
A
(F)
B
(G)
right to take my place in the Hu - man race.
3. And now I know how Joan of
T
A
B

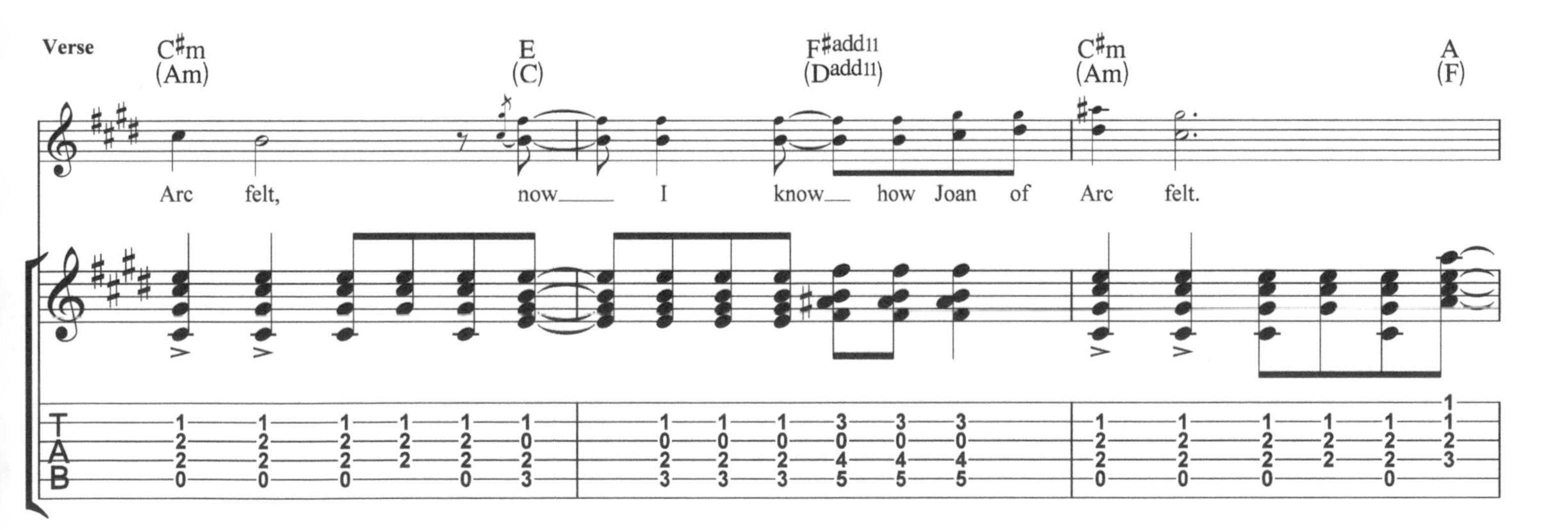
Verse
C♯m
(Am)
E
(C)
F♯add11
(Dadd11)
C♯m
(Am)
A
(F)
Arc felt, now I know how Joan of Arc felt.
T
A
B

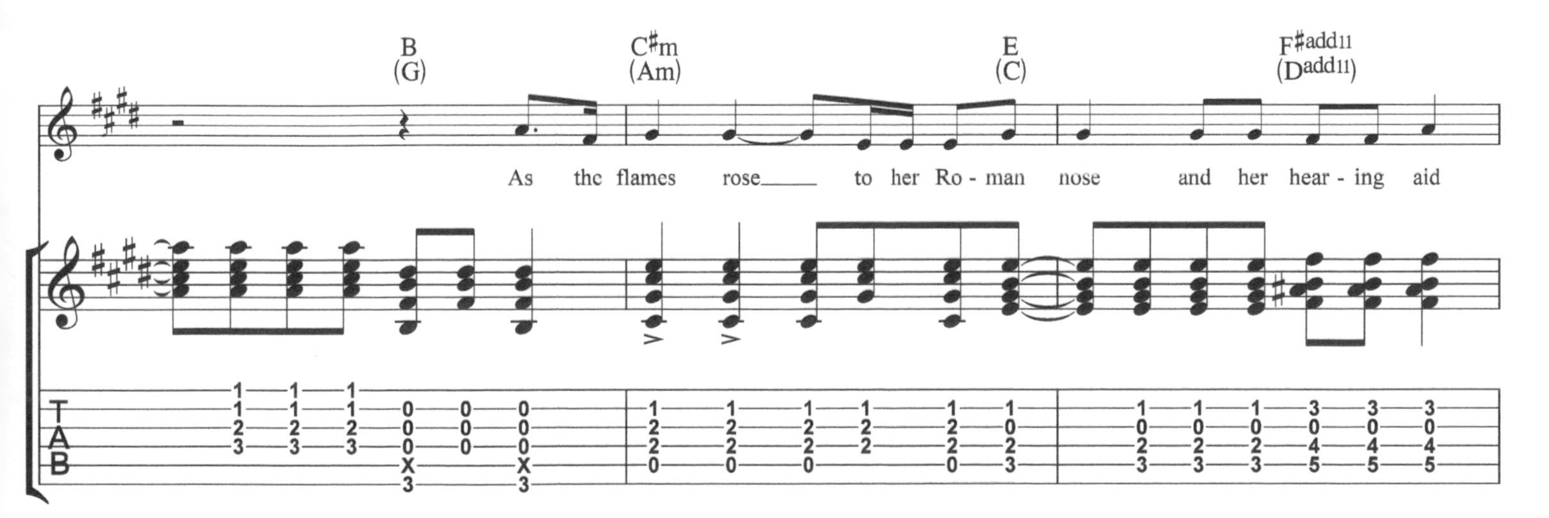
B
(G)
C♯m
(Am)
E
(C)
F♯add11
(Dadd11)
As the flames rose to her Ro - man nose and her hear - ing aid
T
A
B

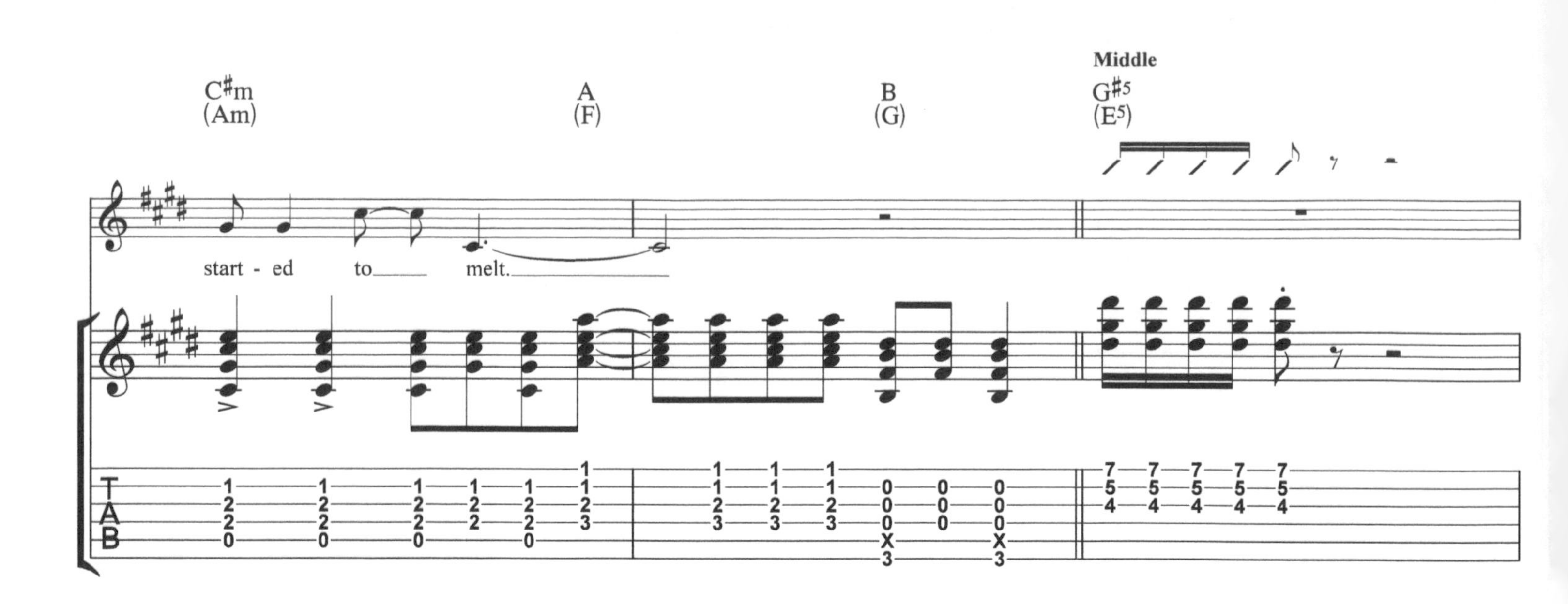
Middle
C♯m
(Am)
A
(F)
B
(G)
G♯5
(E5)
start - ed to melt.

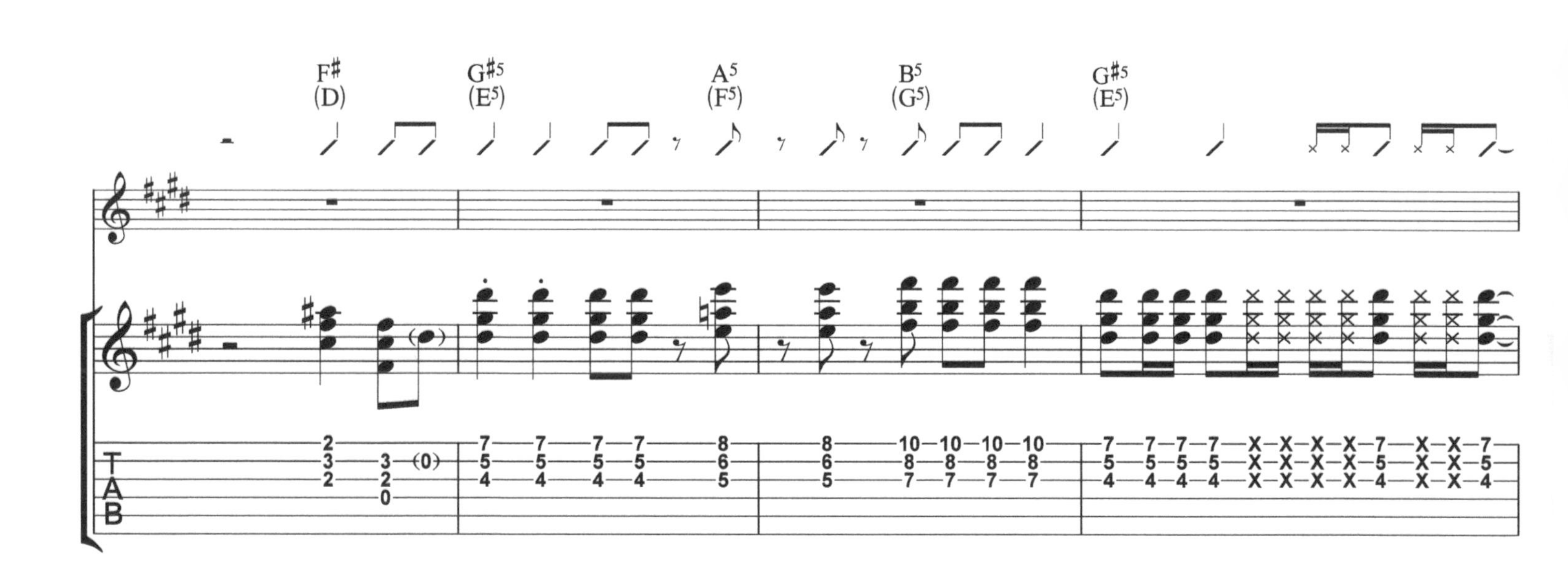
F♯
(D)
G♯5
(E5)
A5
(F5)
B5
(G5)
G♯5
(E5)

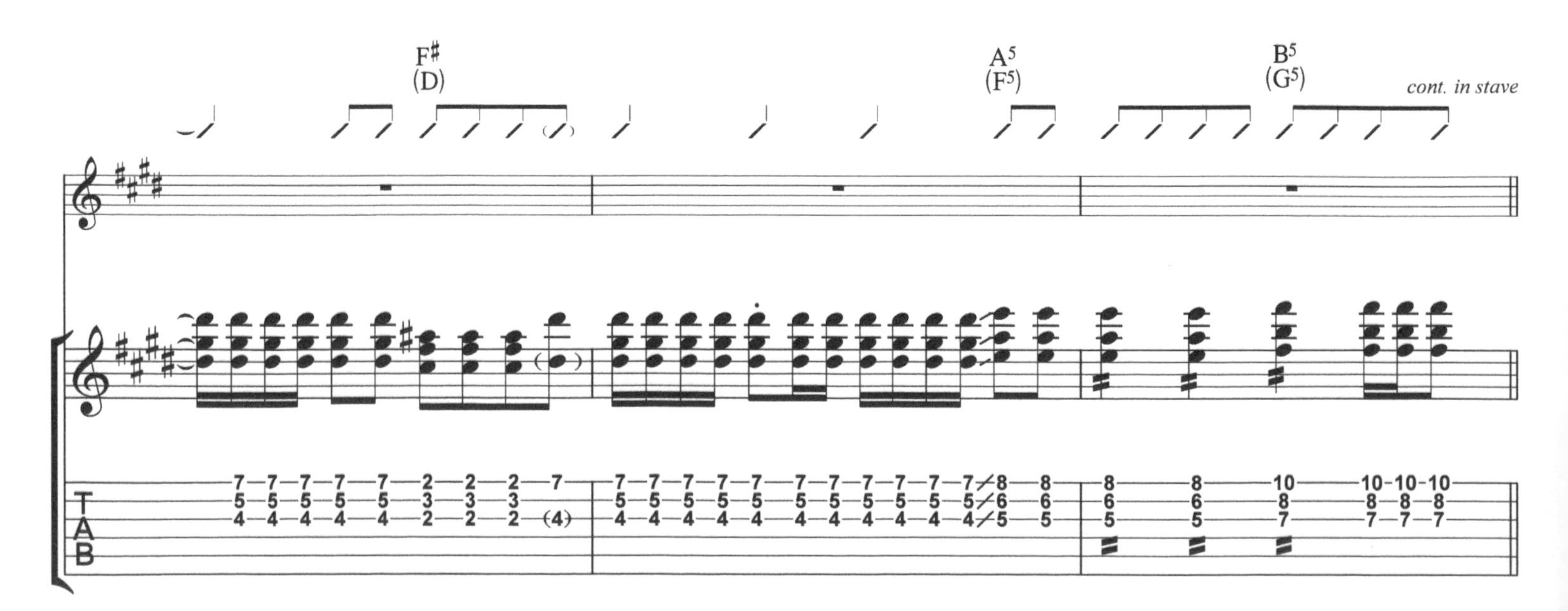
F♯
(D)
A5
(F5)
B5
(G5)
cont. in stave

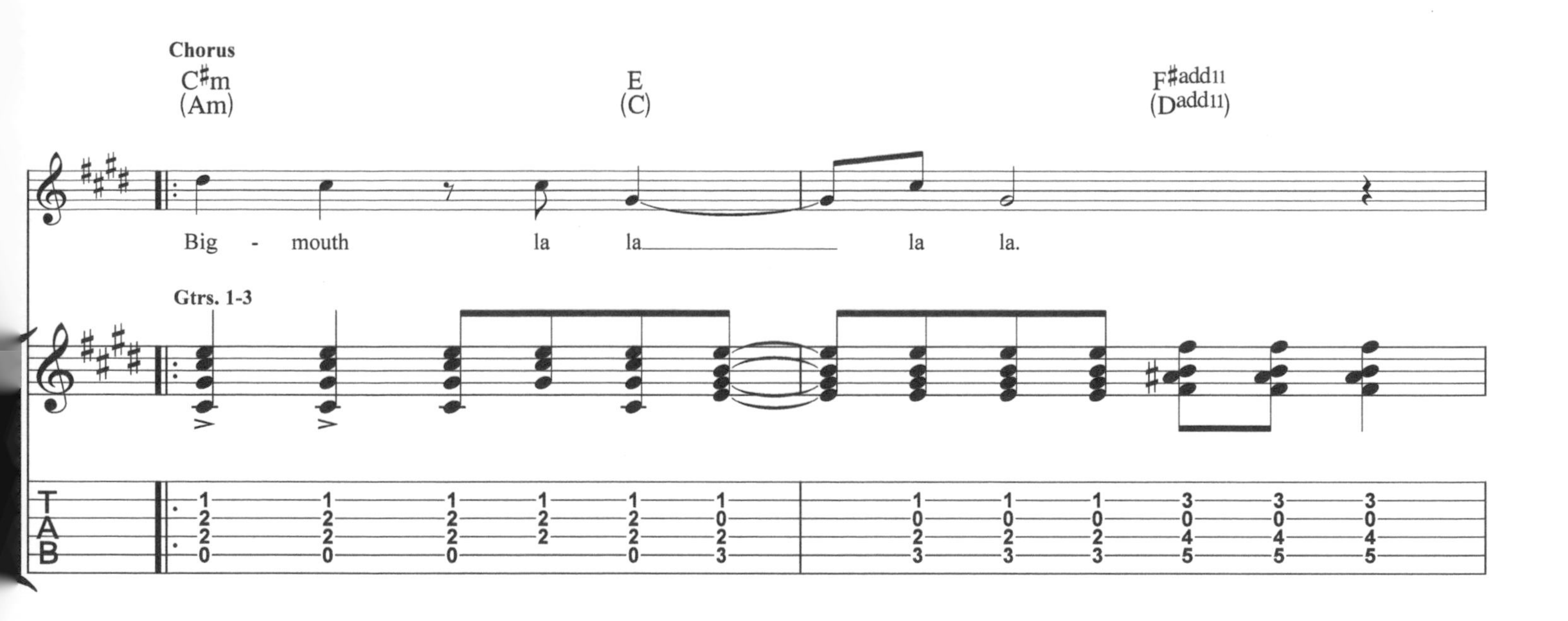
Chorus
C♯m (Am)
E (C)
F♯add11 (Dadd11)
Big - mouth la la la la.
Gtrs. 1-3

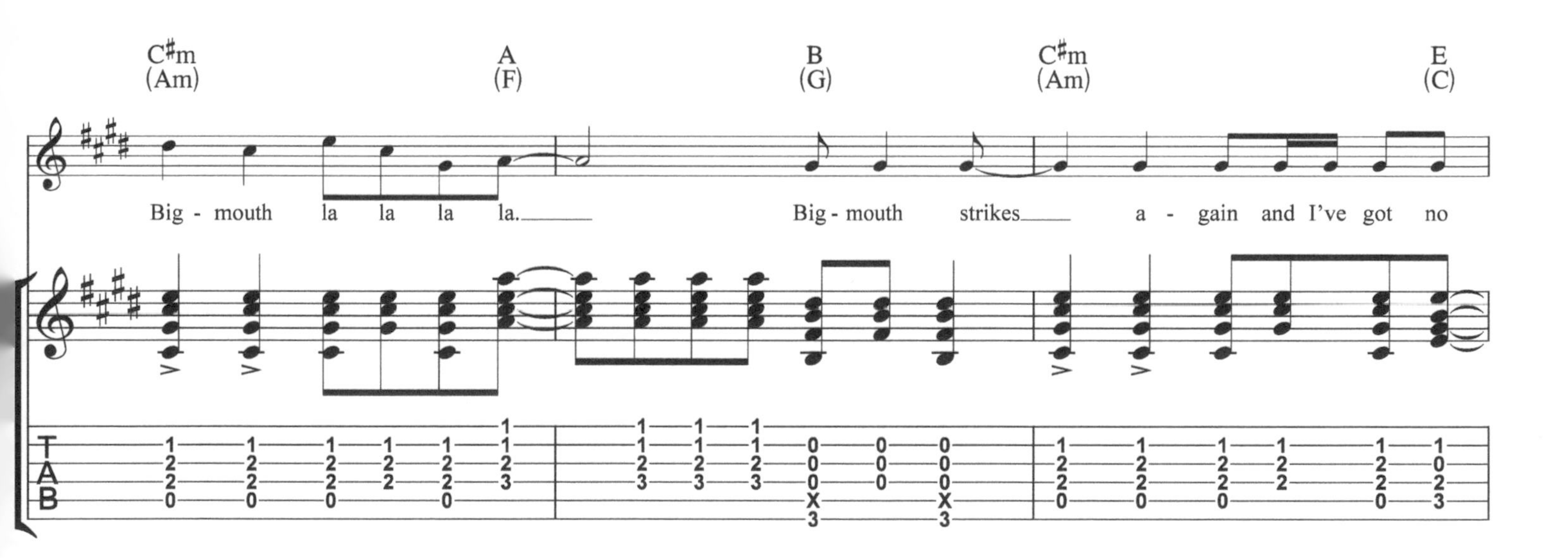
C♯m (Am)
A (F)
B (G)
C♯m (Am)
E (C)
Big - mouth la la la la.
Big - mouth strikes a - gain and I've got no

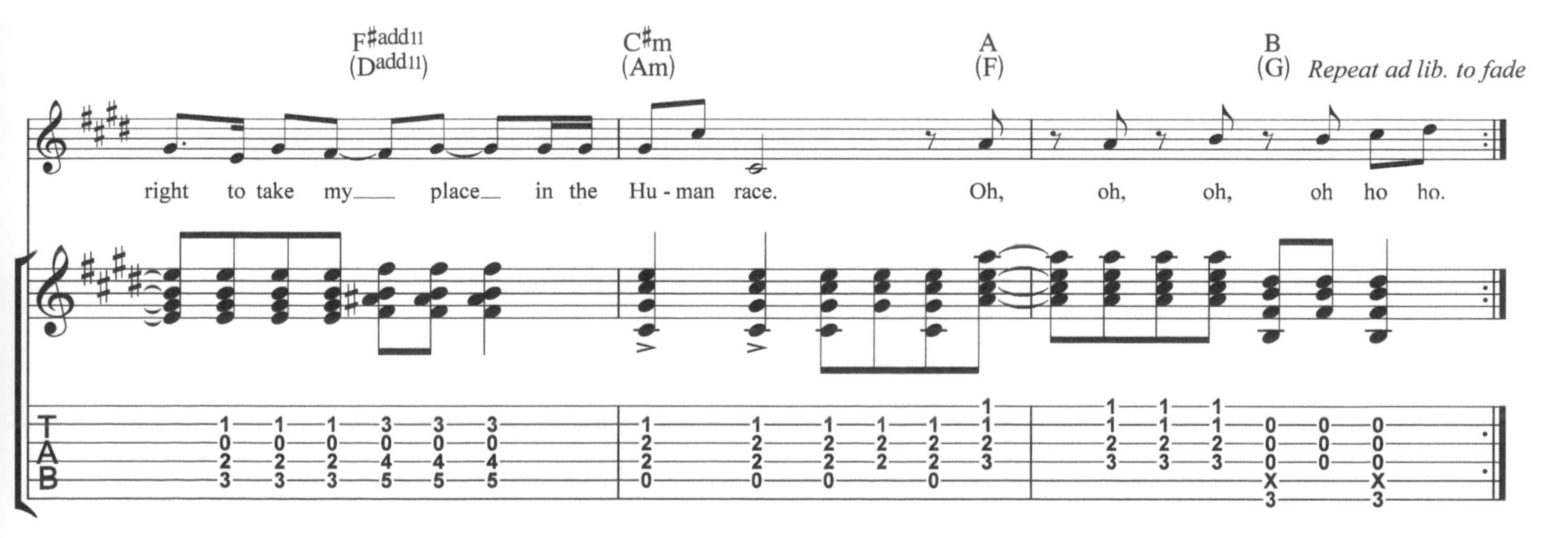
F♯add11 (Dadd11)
C♯m (Am)
A (F)
B (G)
Repeat ad lib. to fade
right to take my place in the Hu - man race.
Oh, oh, oh, oh ho ho.

heaven knows I'm miserable now

Words & Music by Morrissey & Johnny Marr

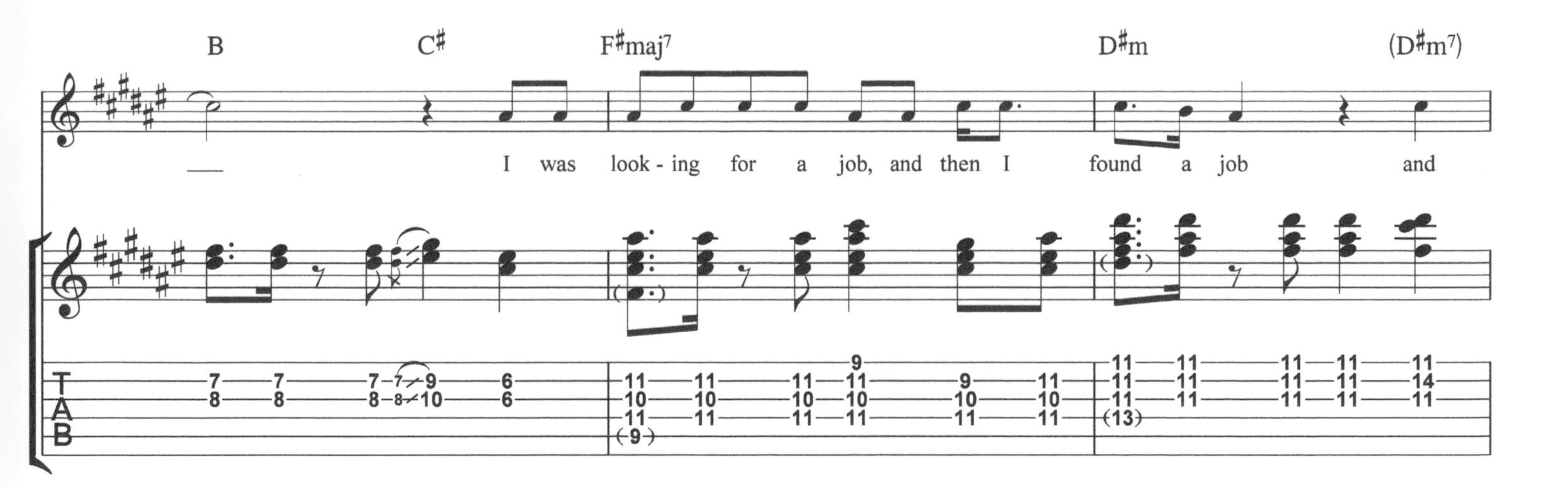
B C♯ F♯maj7 D♯m (D♯m7)
I was look - ing for a job, and then I found a job and

G♯m (G♯m/F♯bass) B C♯ F♯maj7
Hea - ven knows I'm mis - 'ra - ble now. In my life

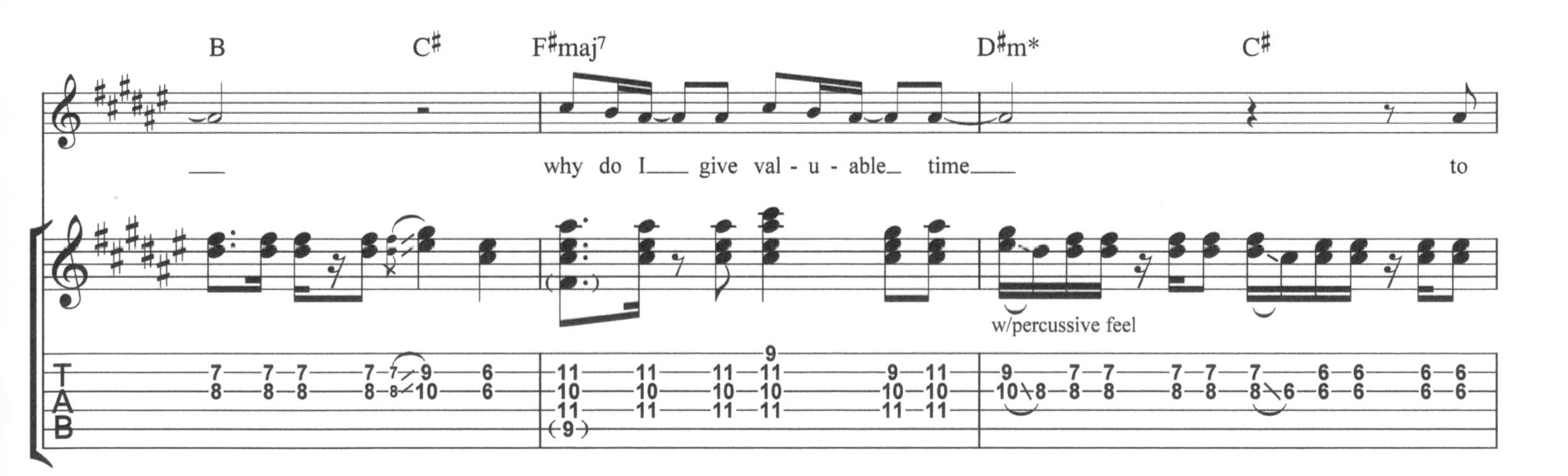
B C♯ F♯maj7 D♯m* C♯
why do I give val - u - able time to
w/percussive feel

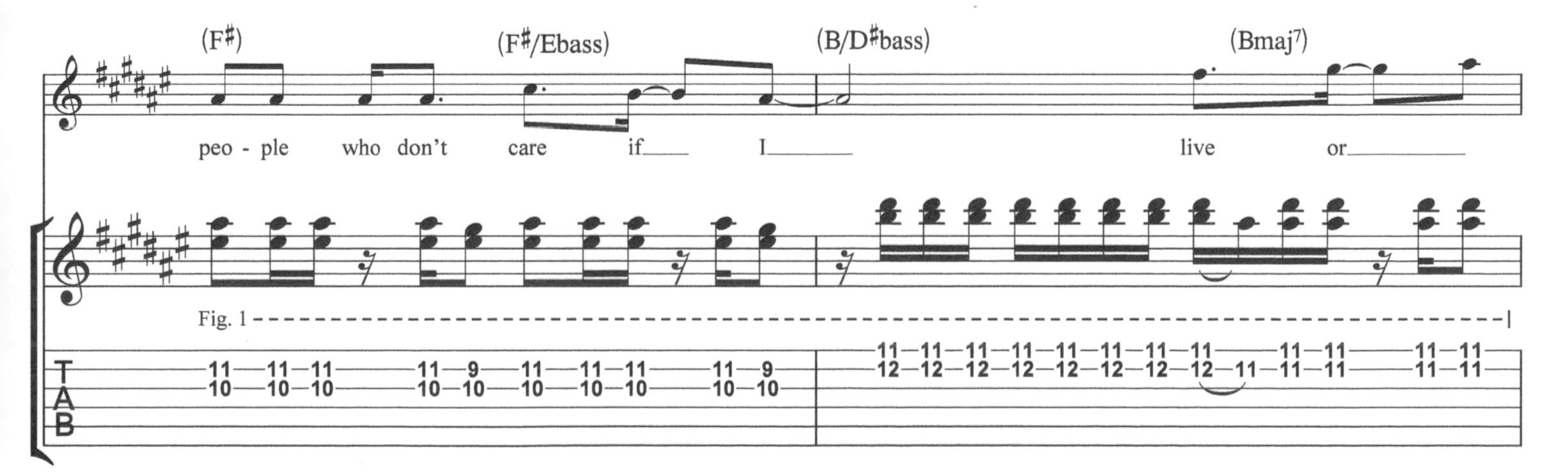
(F♯) (F♯/Ebass) (B/D♯bass) (Bmaj7)
peo - ple who don't care if I live or
Fig. 1

(B/D♯bass)
(C♯/E♯bass)
(B/D♯bass)
(C♯)
die?
Gtr. 3 (elec.)
f
(F♯)
(F♯/Ebass)
(B/D♯bass) (Bmaj7)
B
C
C♯
2. Two
8va
Gtrs. 1+2 w/Fig. 1
Gtr. 3 w/bright clean tone
Gtrs. 1+2 cont in slashes
Verse
*F♯5(♯7)
D♯madd9
G♯m*
G♯m/F♯
C♯sus4
lov - ers en - twined
pass me by
and Hea - ven knows I'm mis-'ra - ble now.
I was
mp
*Gtrs. 1+2 w/♪ picking using above chord names
look - ing for a job, and then I found a job and Hea - ven knows I'm mis-'ra - ble now.

*F♯5(♯7)
D♯madd9
G♯m*
G♯m/F♯
C♯sus4
In my life oh, why do I give val-u-able time to

*F♯5(♯7)
D♯madd9
G♯m*
G♯m/F♯
C♯sus4
peo-ple who don't care if I live or die?

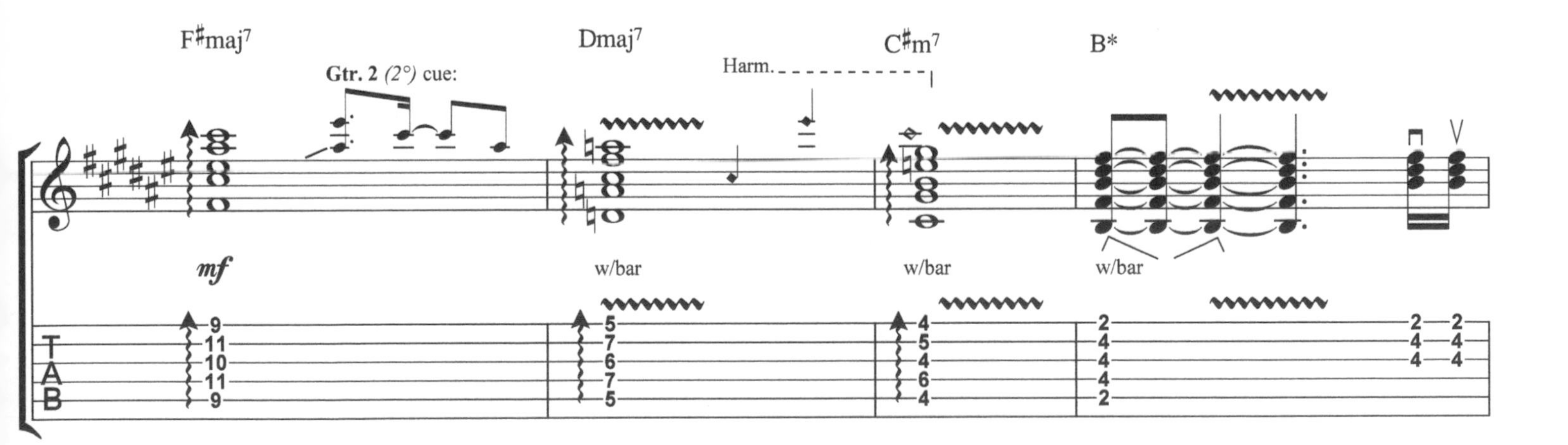
F♯maj7
Dmaj7
C♯m7
B*
Gtr. 2 (2°) cue:
Harm.
mf
w/bar
w/bar
w/bar

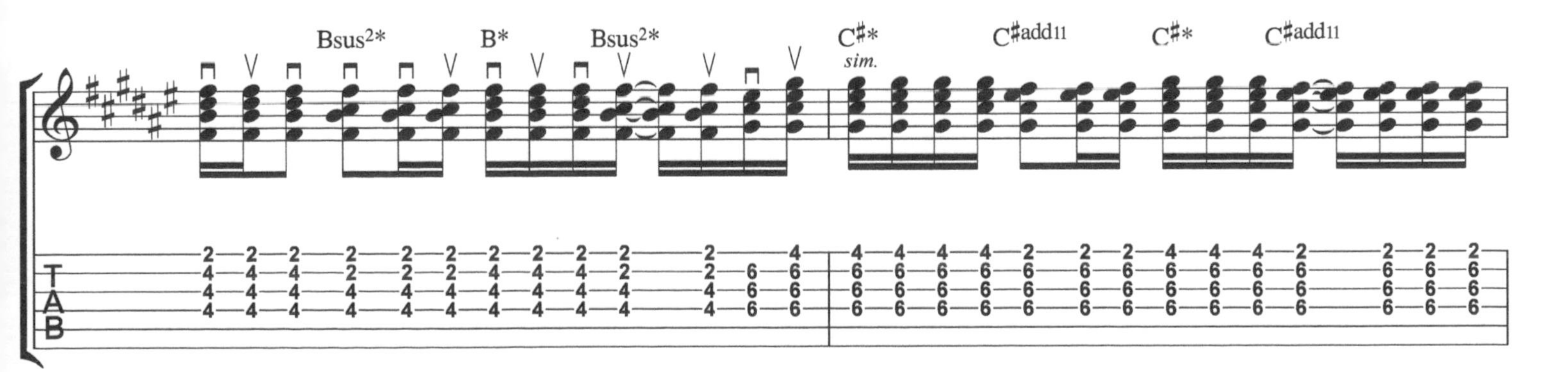
Bsus2*
B*
Bsus2*
C♯*
C♯add11
C♯*
C♯add11
sim.

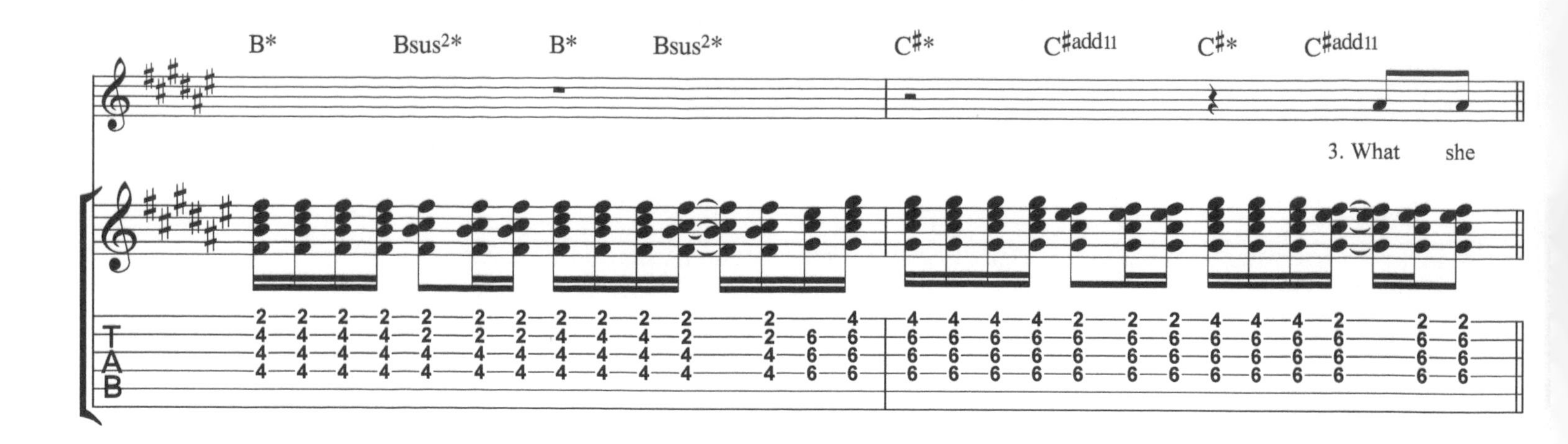
B*
Bsus2*
B*
Bsus2*
C#*
C#add11
C#*
C#add11
3. What she
T
A
B

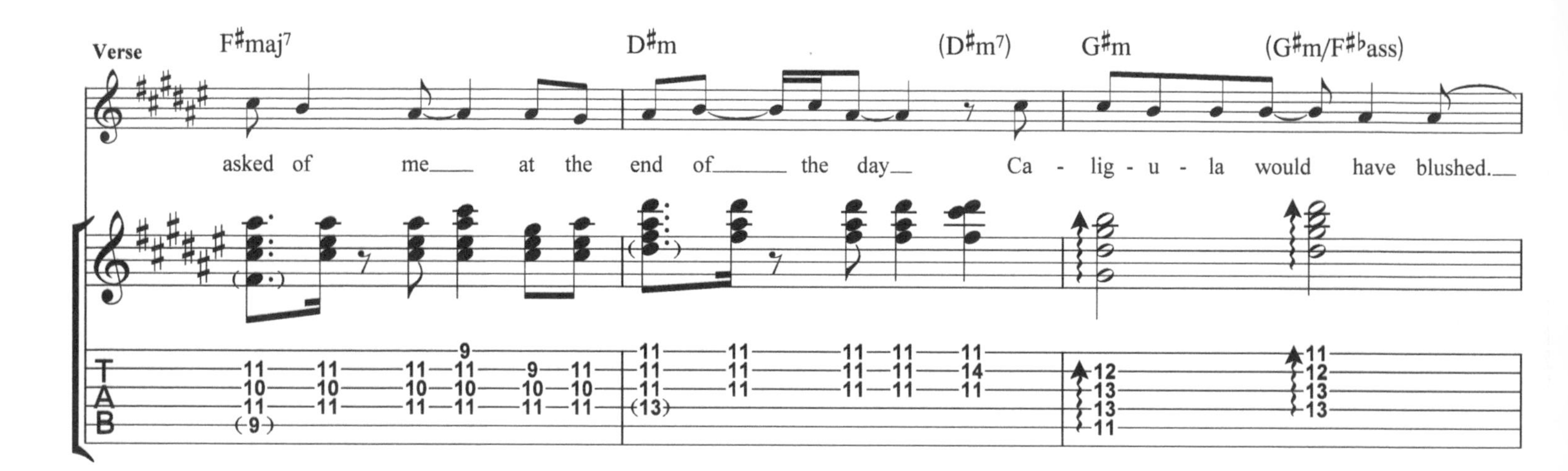
Verse
F#maj7
D#m
(D#m7)
G#m
(G#m/F#bass)
asked of me at the end of the day Ca - lig - u - la would have blushed.

B
C#
*F#5(#7)
D#madd9
"Oh, you've been in the house too long" she said and I

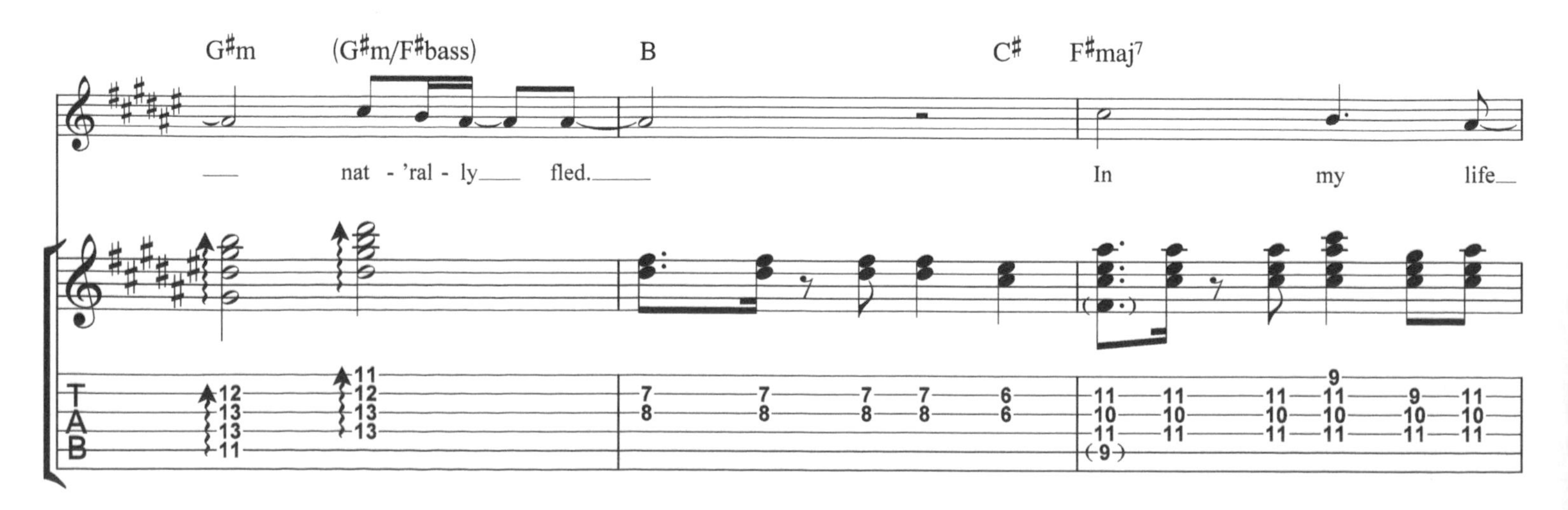
G#m
(G#m/F#bass)
B
C#
F#maj7
nat - 'ral - ly fled.
In my life

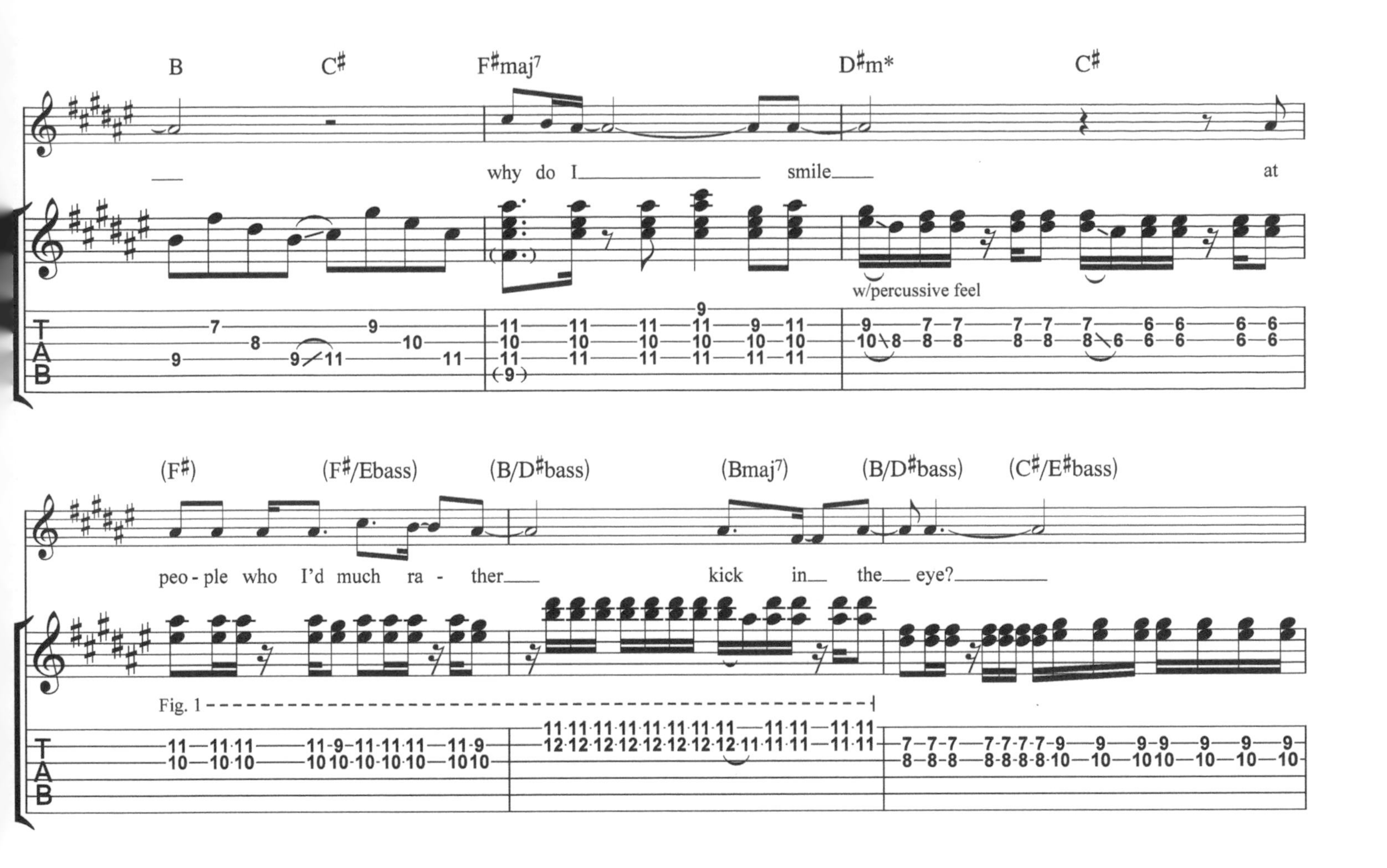
B
C#
F#maj7
D#m*
C#
why do I smile at
w/percussive feel
(F#)
(F#/Ebass)
(B/D#bass)
(Bmaj7)
(B/D#bass)
(C#/E#bass)
peo - ple who I'd much ra - ther kick in the eye?
Fig. 1

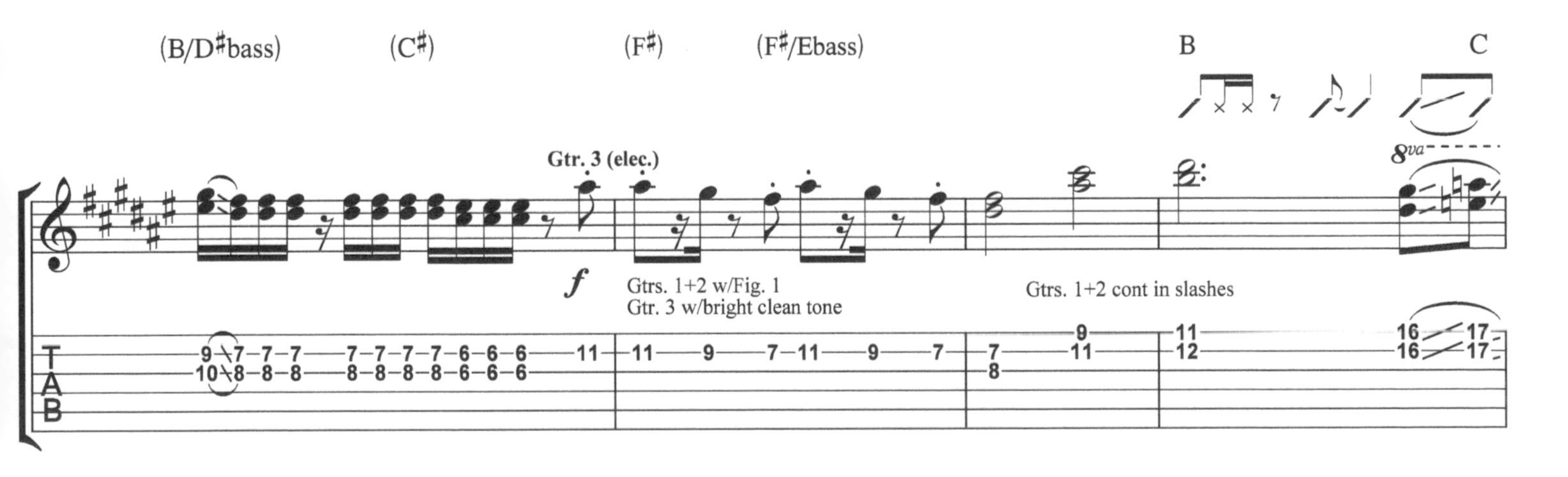
(B/D#bass)
(C#)
(F#)
(F#/Ebass)
B
C
Gtr. 3 (elec.)
f
Gtrs. 1+2 w/Fig. 1
Gtr. 3 w/bright clean tone
Gtrs. 1+2 cont in slashes
8va

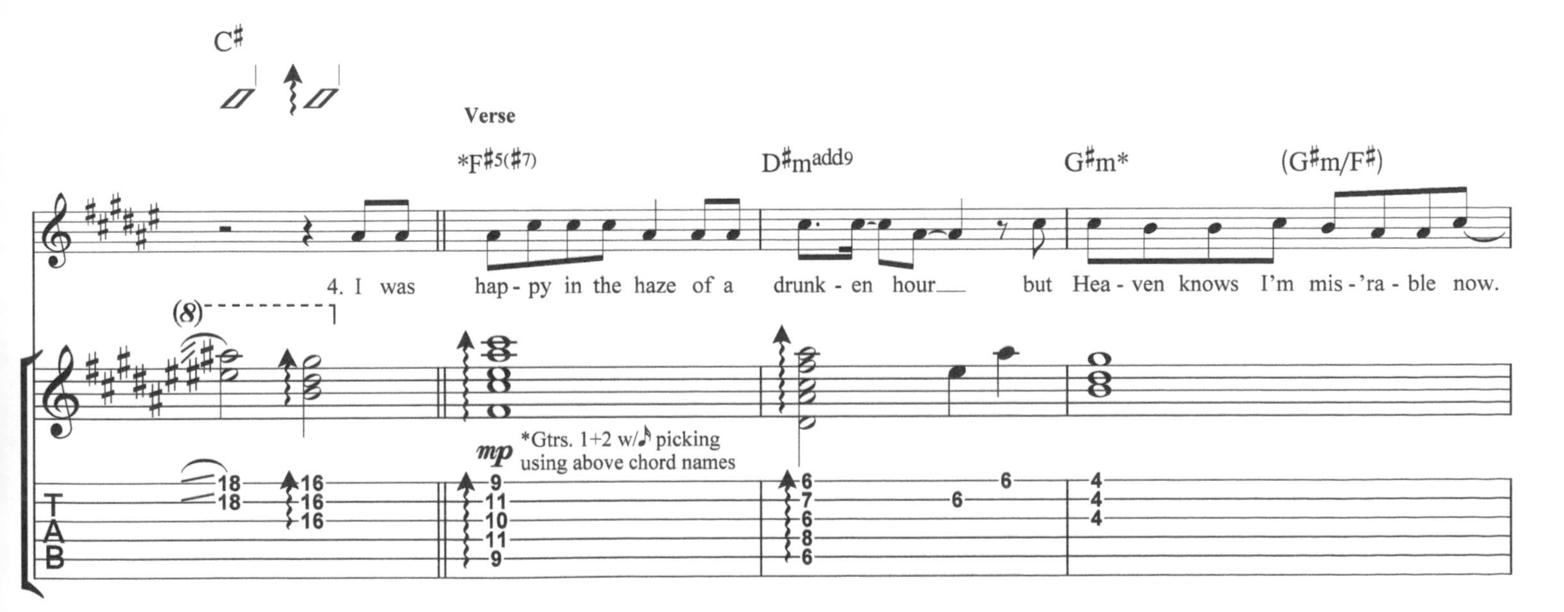
C#
Verse
*F#5(#7)
D#madd9
G#m*
(G#m/F#)
4. I was hap - py in the haze of a drunk - en hour but Hea - ven knows I'm mis - 'ra - ble now.
(8)
mp
*Gtrs. 1+2 w/♪ picking
using above chord names

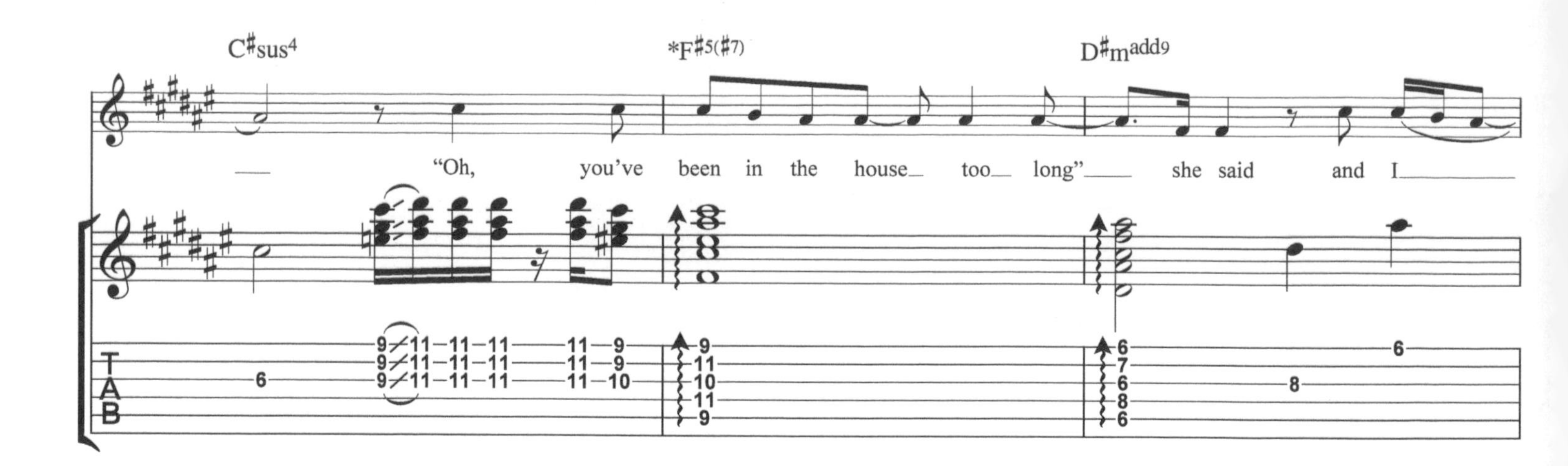
C♯sus4
*F♯5(♯7)
D♯madd9
"Oh, you've been in the house too long" she said and I

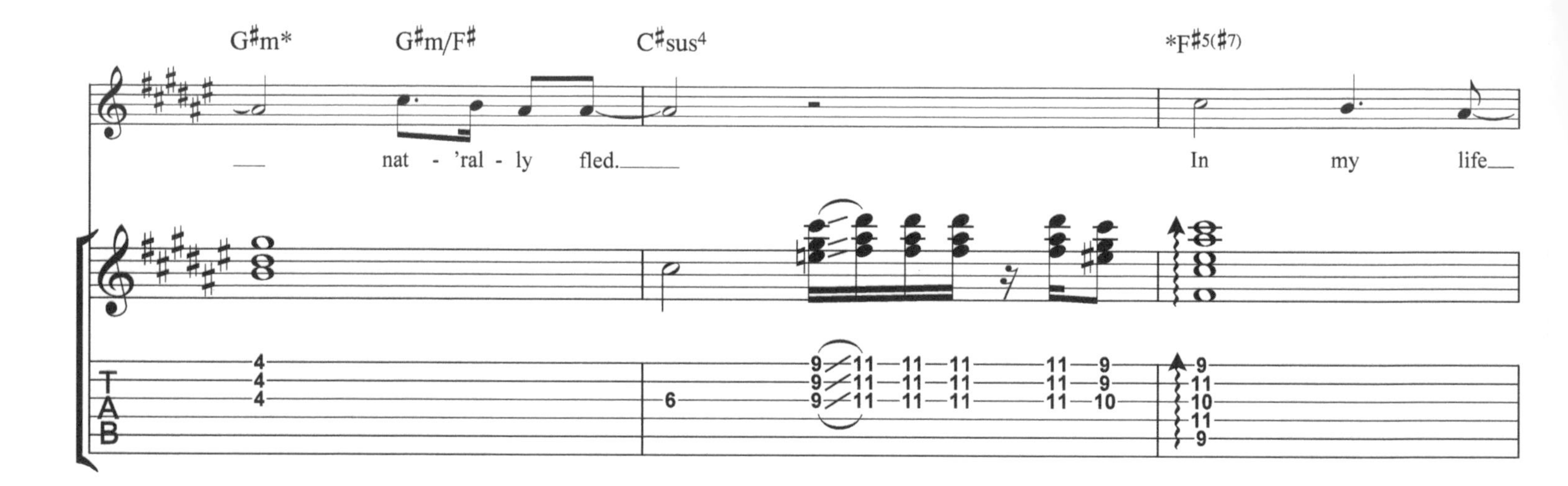
G♯m*
G♯m/F♯
C♯sus4
*F♯5(♯7)
nat - 'ral - ly fled. In my life

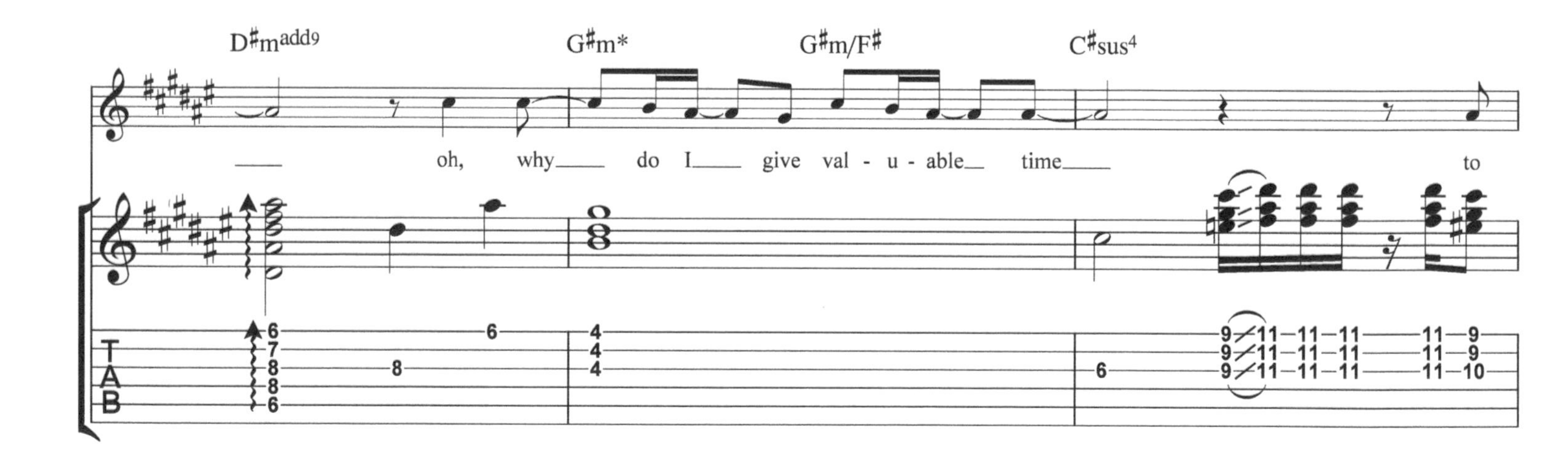
D♯madd9
G♯m*
G♯m/F♯
C♯sus4
oh, why do I give val - u - able time to

*F♯5(♯7)
D♯madd9
G♯m*
G♯m/F♯
C♯sus4
peo - ple who don't care if I live or die?

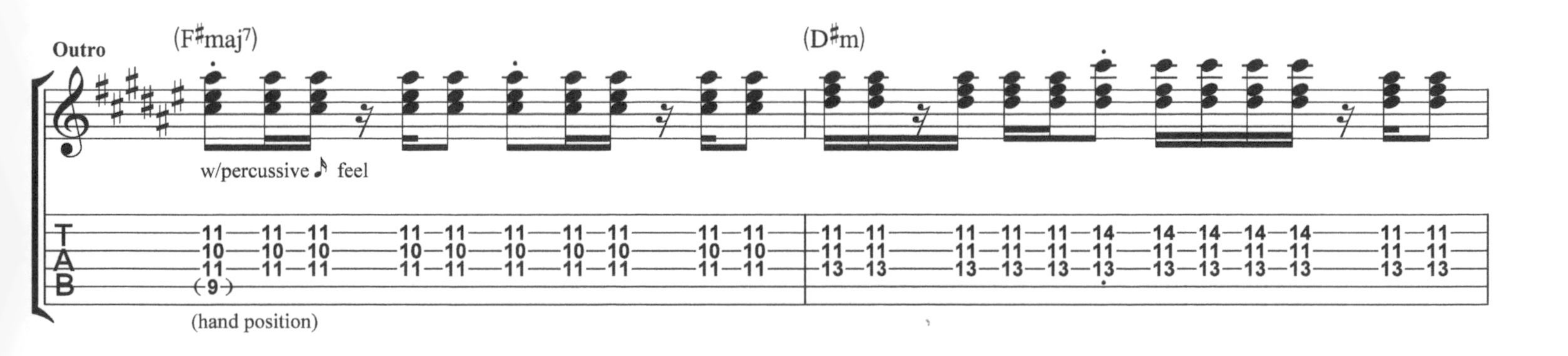
Outro
(F#maj7)
(D#m)
w/percussive feel
(hand position)

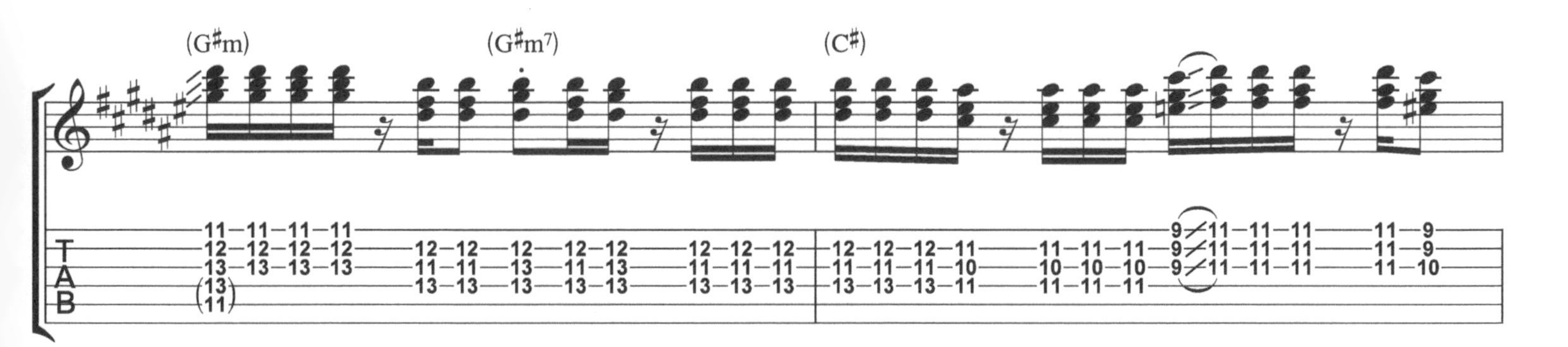
(G#m)
(G#m7)
(C#)

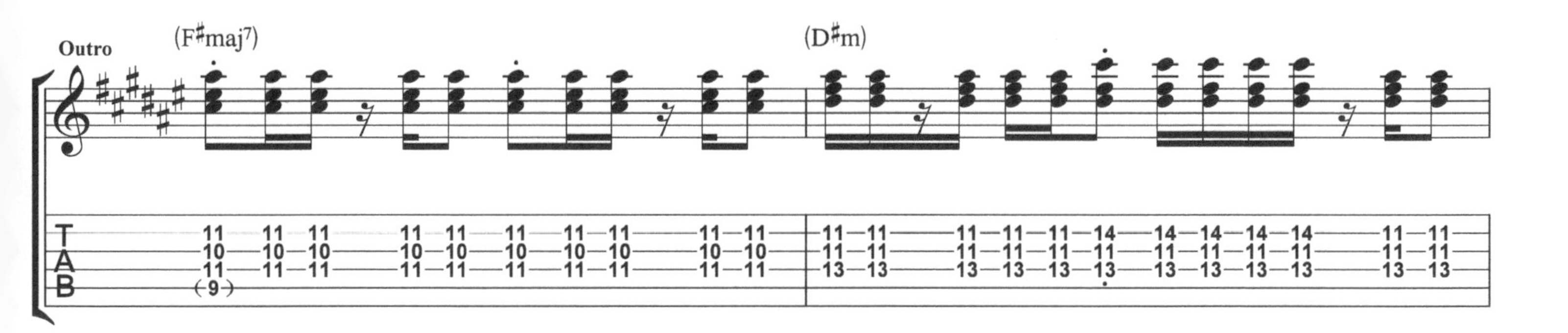
Outro
(F#maj7)
(D#m)

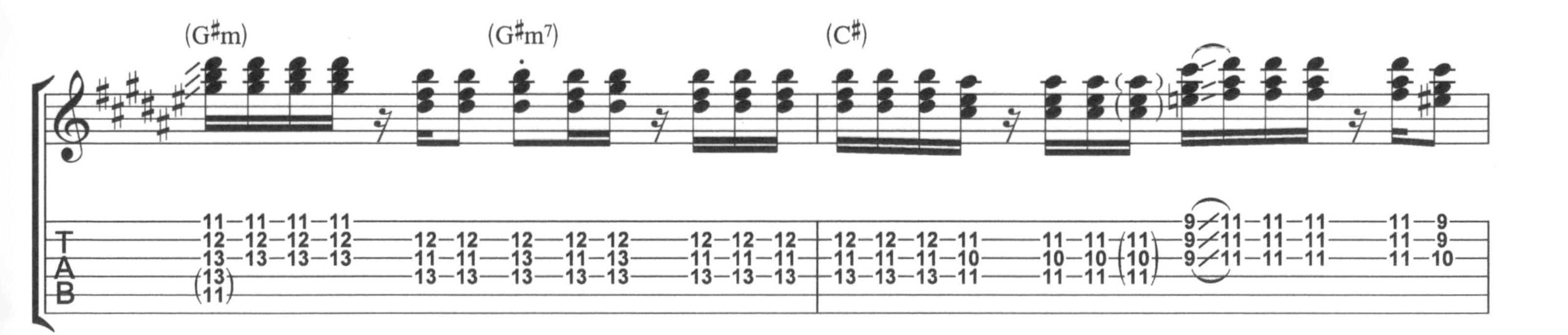
(G#m)
(G#m7)
(C#)

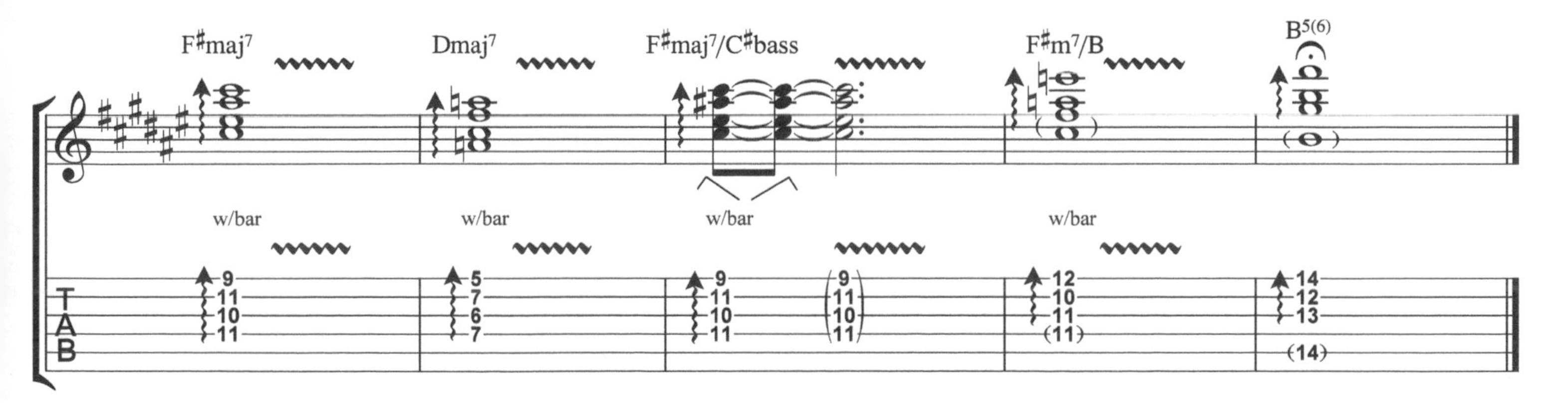
F#maj7
Dmaj7
F#maj7/C#bass
F#m7/B
B5(6)
w/bar
w/bar
w/bar
w/bar

Words & Music by Morrissey & Johnny Marr

D F5 G (Gtr. 3 G5) D Em
cont. sim.
could life ev - er be sane a - gain, on the

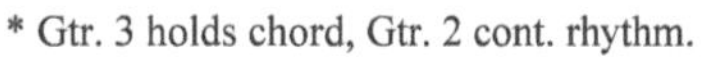
* Gtr. 3 holds chord, Gtr. 2 cont. rhythm.

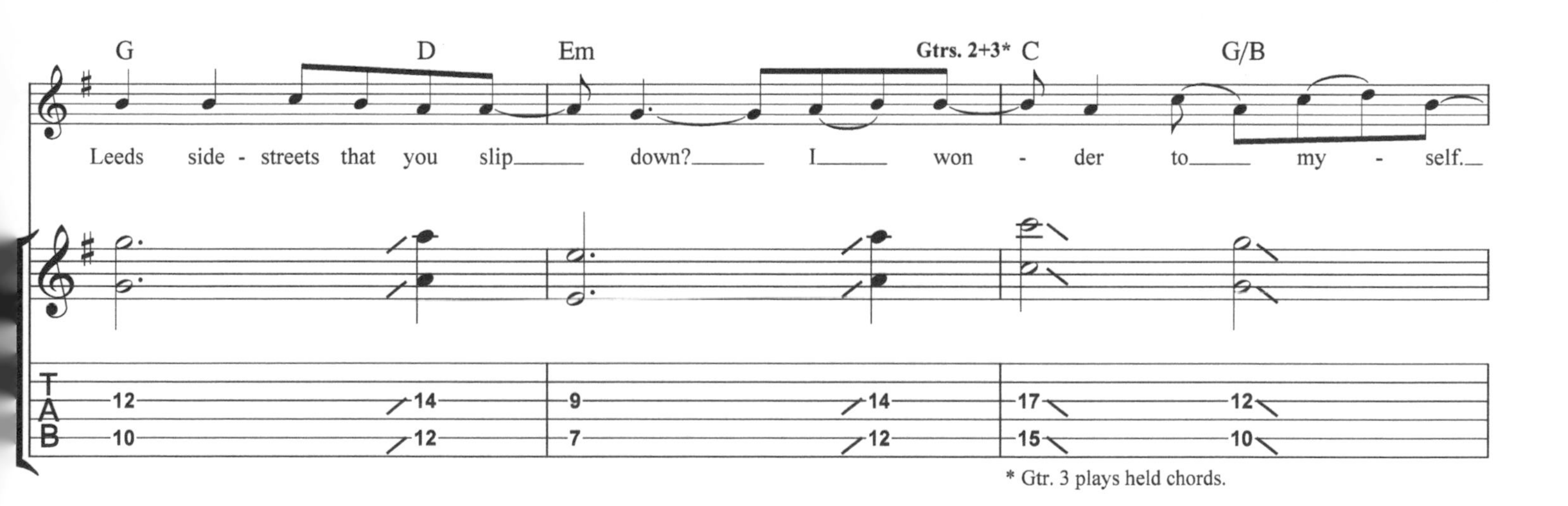
G D Em Gtrs. 2+3* C G/B
Leeds side - streets that you slip down? I won - der to my - self.
* Gtr. 3 plays held chords.

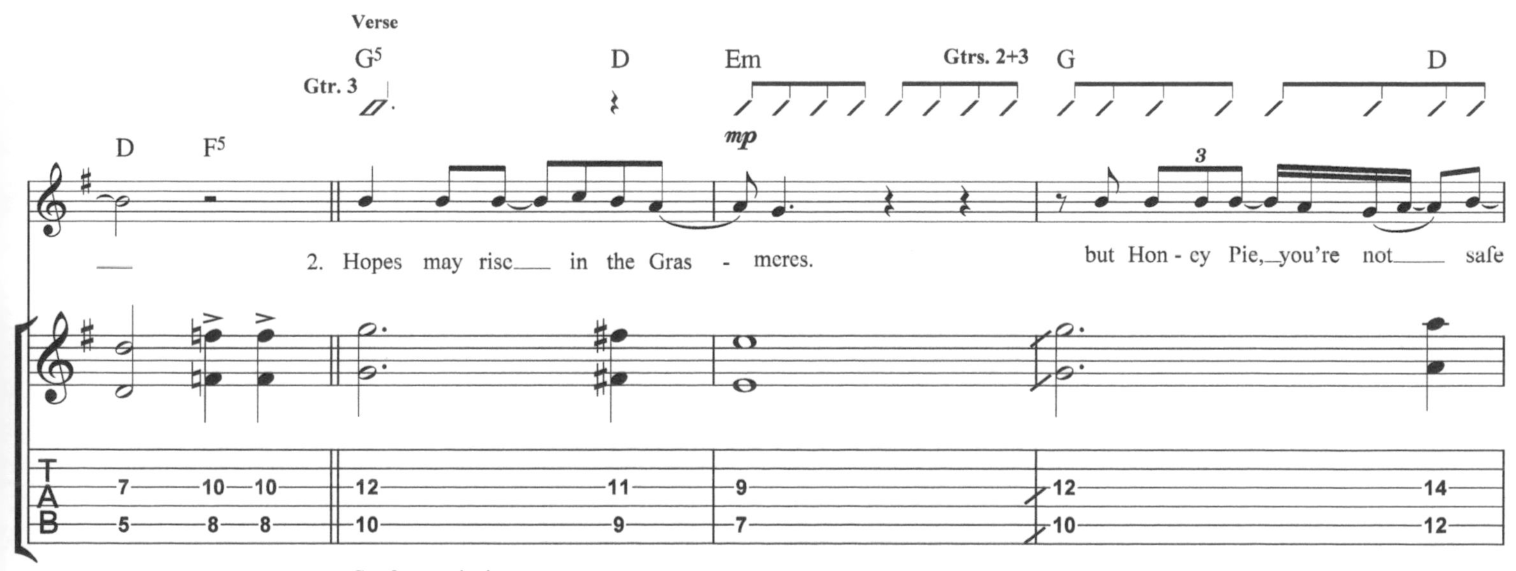
Verse
G5 D Em Gtrs. 2+3 G D
Gtr. 3
D F5
mp
2. Hopes may rise in the Gras - meres.
but Hon - ey Pie, you're not safe
Gtr. 2 cont. rhythm

Gtr. 2+3*
Em
C
G/B
D
F5
cont. sim.
here, so you run down to the safe - ty of the town. But there's
* Gtr. 3 plays held chords (see chord boxes)
G (Gtr. 3 G5)
Em
G
D
pa - nic on the streets of Car - lisle, Dub - lin, Dun - dee, Hum -
* Gtr. 3 holds chord, Gtr. 2 cont. rhythm.
Em
C
13fr
(G/B)
D
10fr
F5
Gtr. 3
- ber - side. I won - der to my - self.
Gtr. 3 w/slide + sustain
Bridge
G
12fr
(E5)
B♭
11fr
B
12fr
C♯
14fr
D
15fr
D♯
16fr
Gtrs. 1+2
Gtr. 2 w/ad lib. picking

E ② 17fr
B♭ ② 11fr
B ② 12fr
C♯ ② 14fr
D ② 15fr
G D Em G D Em
Gtr. 2
cont. sim.
3. Burn down the dis - co, hang the bless - ed D. J. be - cause the
Gtr. 3 tacet
* Gtrs. 2 + 3
C G/B D G (Gtr. 3 G5) D Em
even ♪s
mu - sic that they con - stant - ly play, it says no - thing to me a - bout my life.
* Gtr. 3 plays held chords (see chords boxes)
G (Gtr. 3 G5) D Em C G/B D F5
Hang the bless - ed D. J. be - cause the mu - sic they con - stant - ly play on the

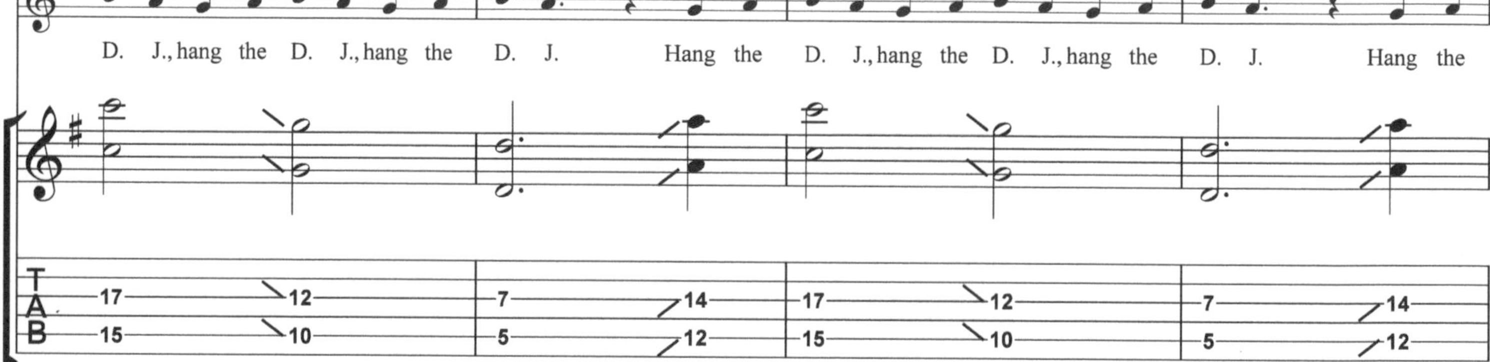

*Gtr. 3 plays held chords

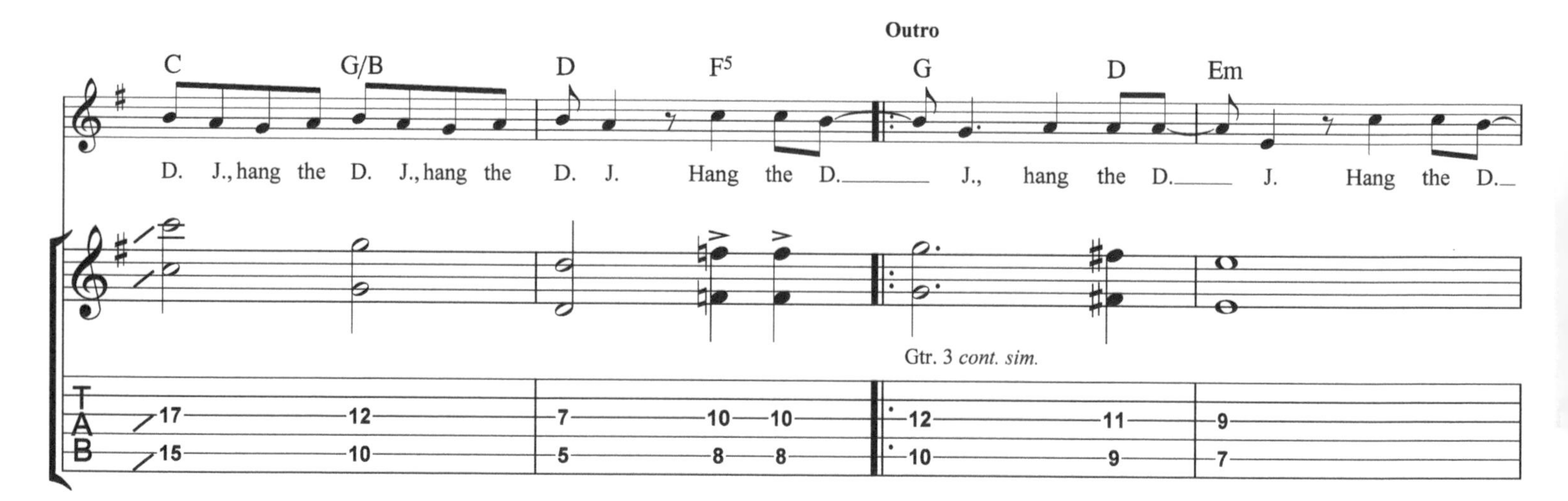

the boy with the thorn in his side

Words & Music by Morrissey & Johnny Marr

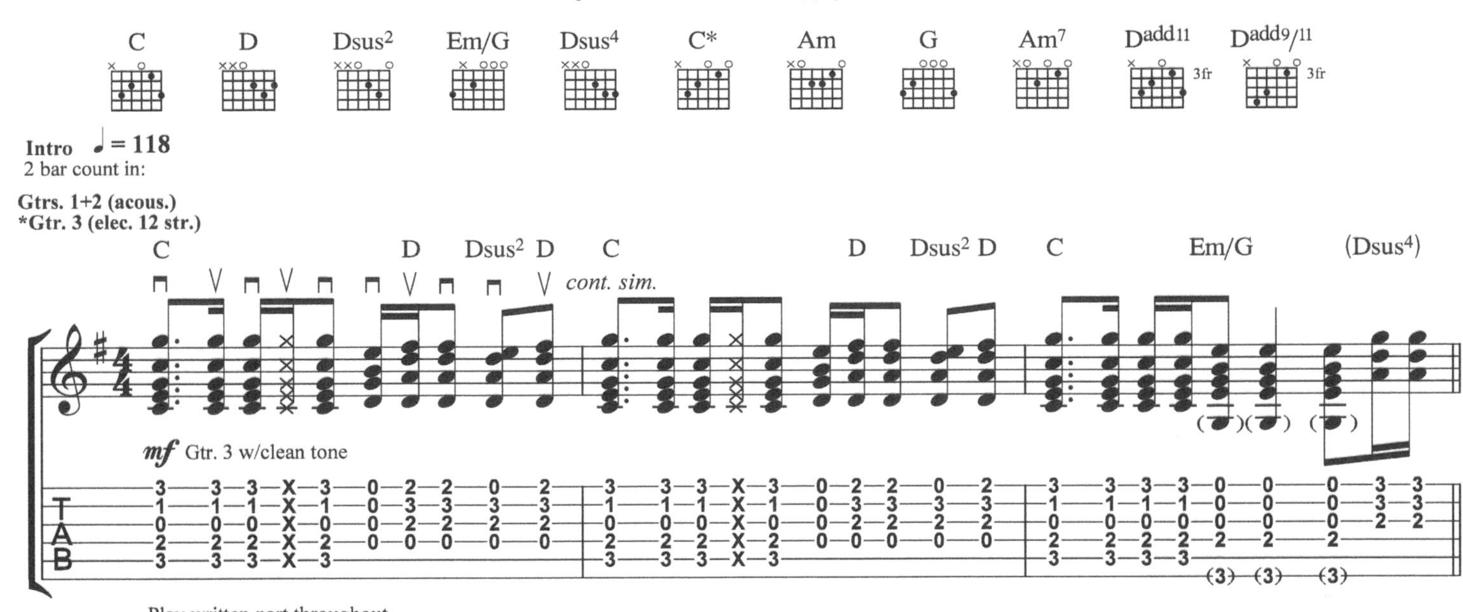

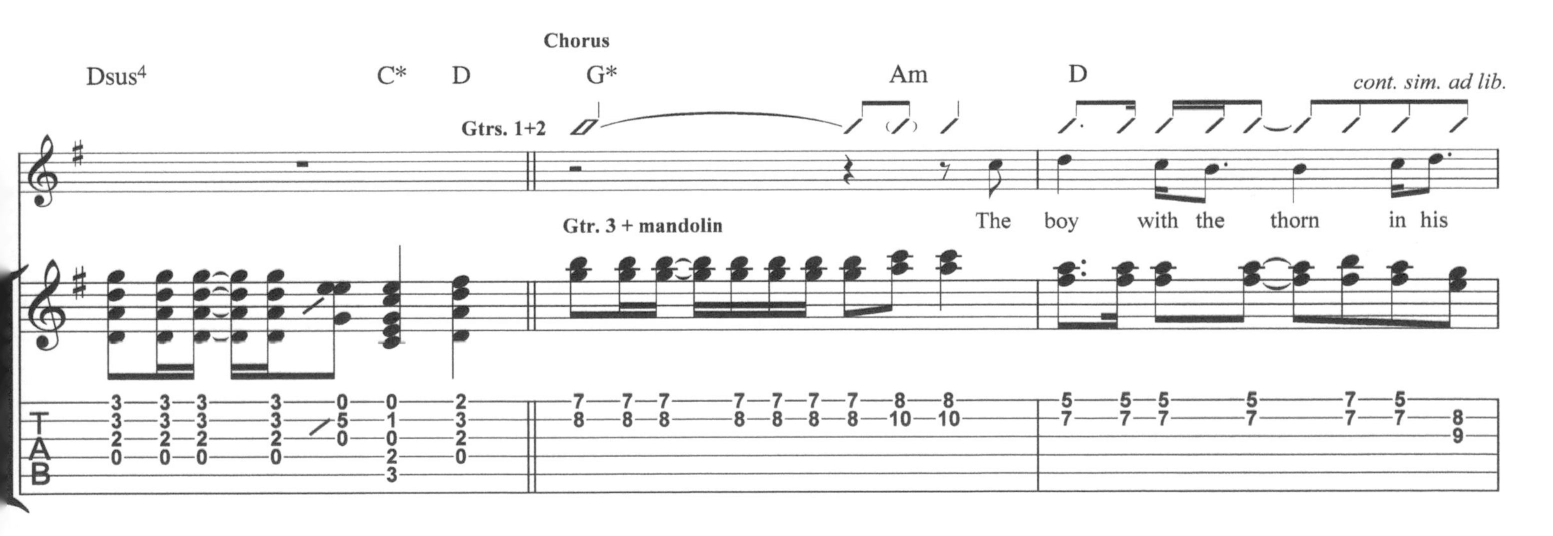

D
Am
for
love.

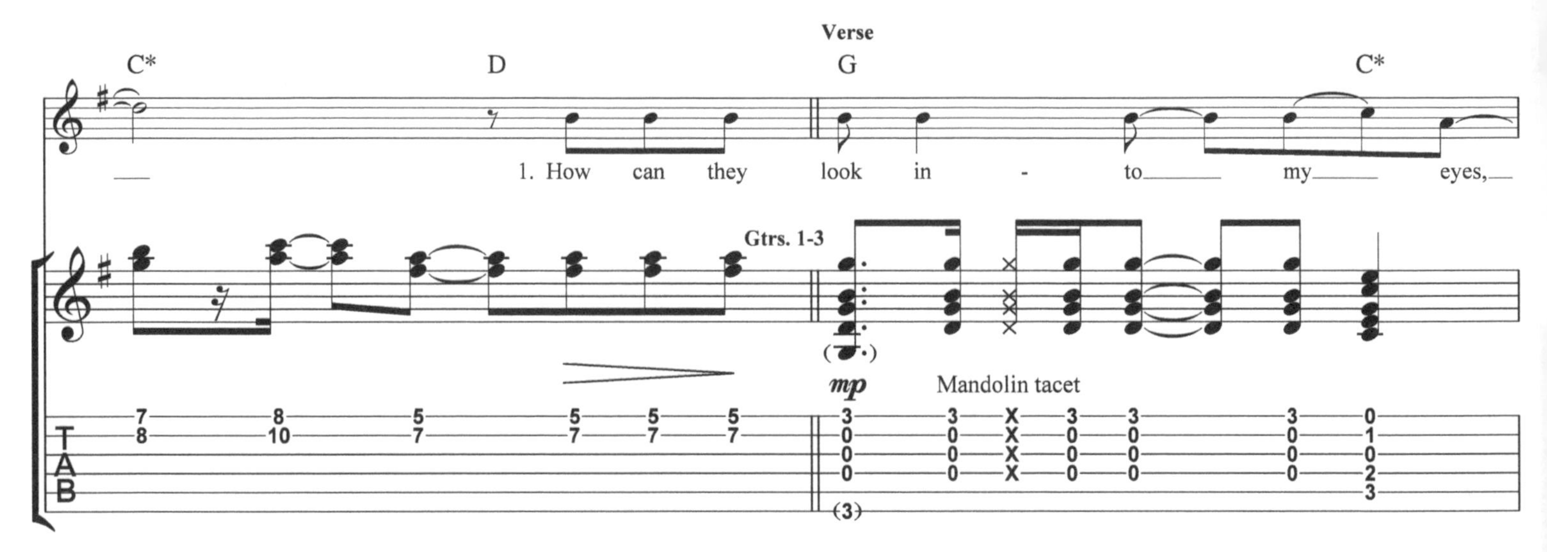
Verse
C*
D
G
C*
1. How can they look in - to my eyes,
Gtrs. 1-3
mp
Mandolin tacet

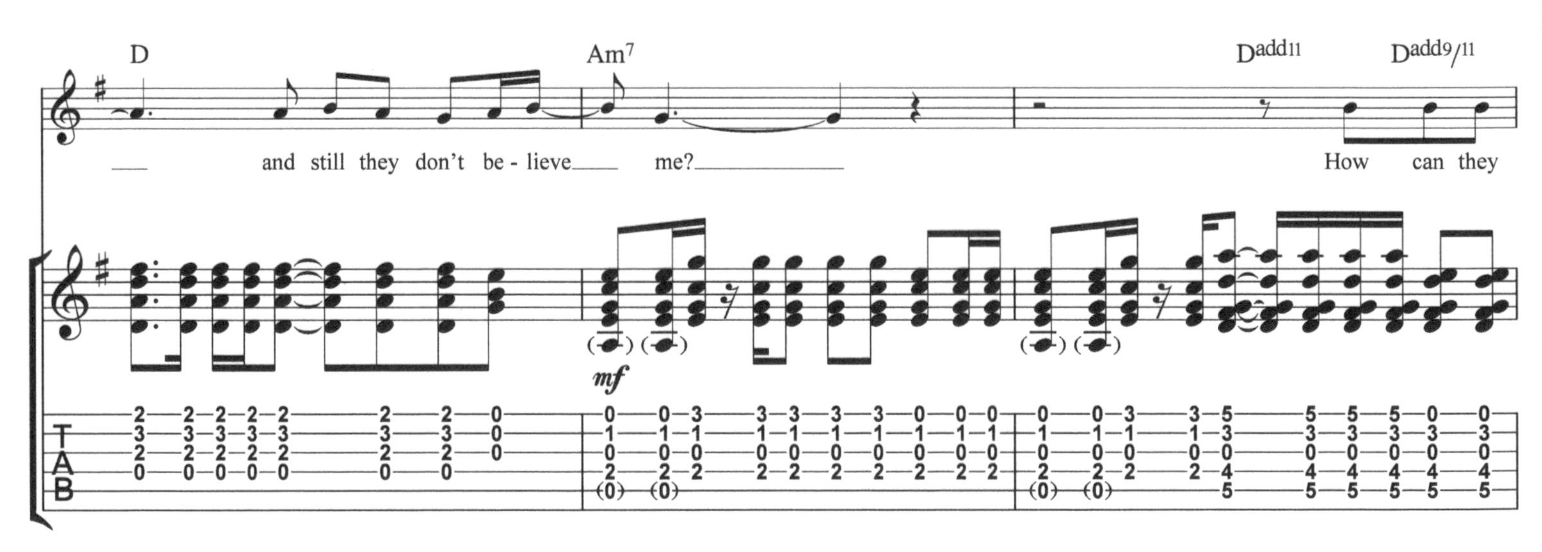
D
Am7
Dadd11
Dadd9/11
and still they don't be - lieve me?
How can they
mf

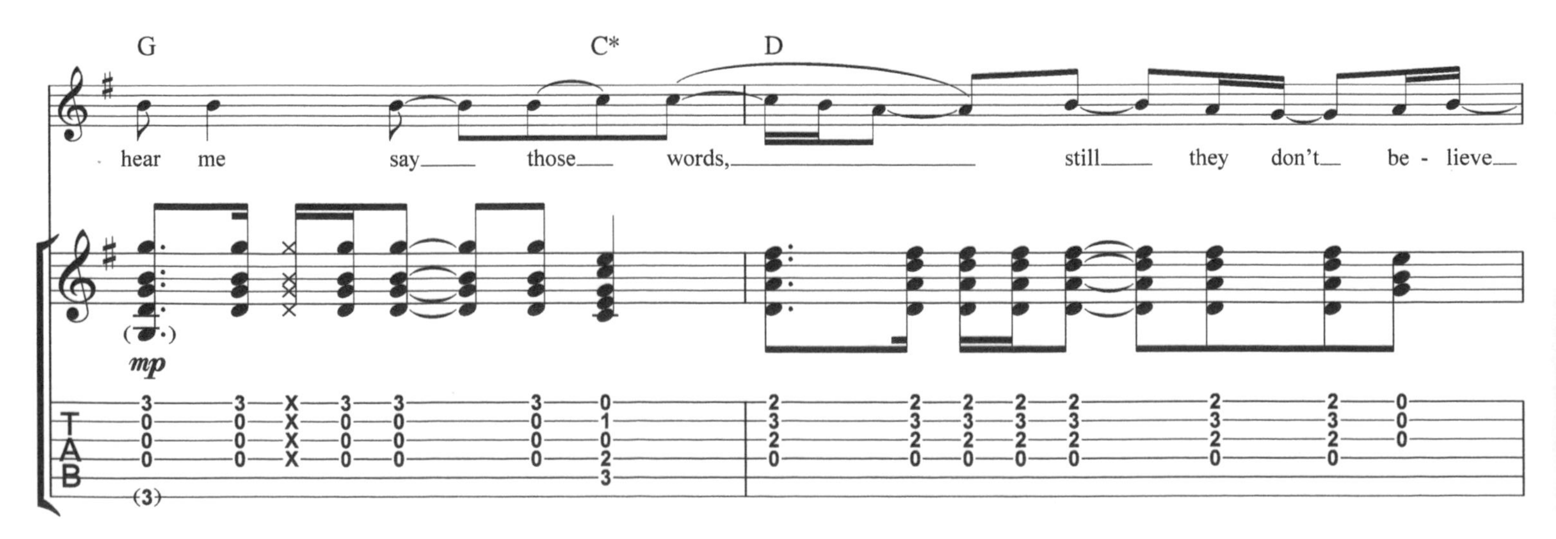
G
C*
D
hear me say those words,
still they don't be - lieve
mp

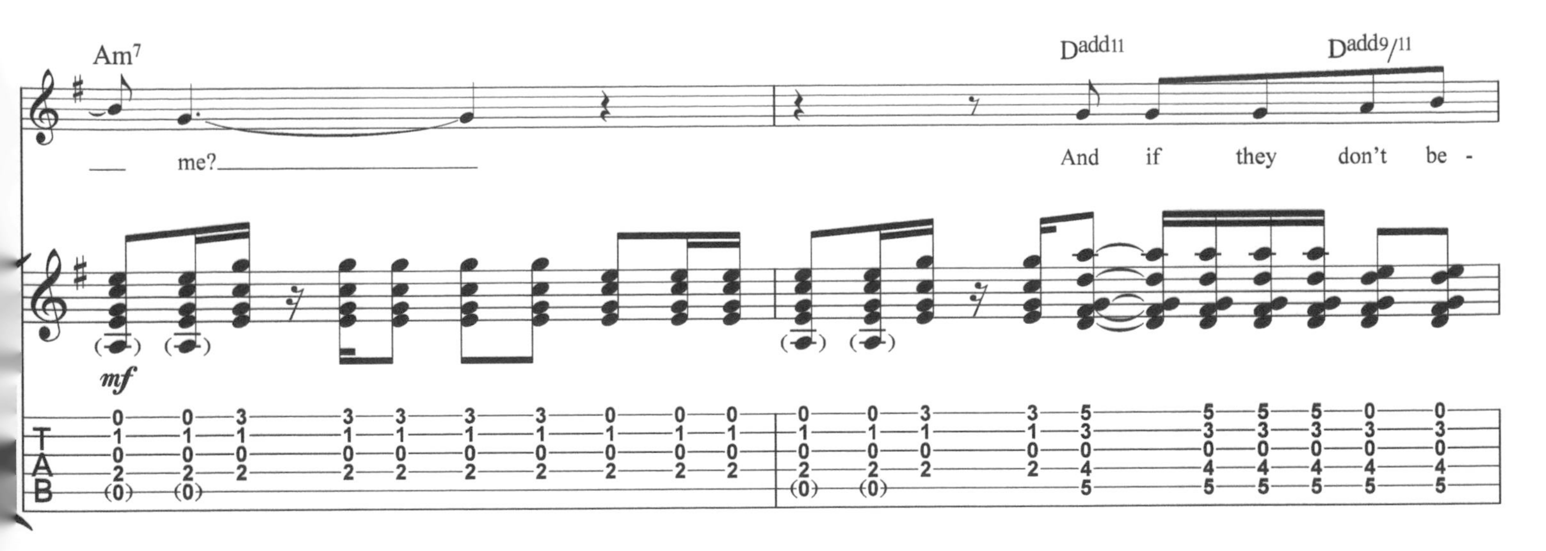
Am7
Dadd11
Dadd9/11
me?
And if they don't be -
mf

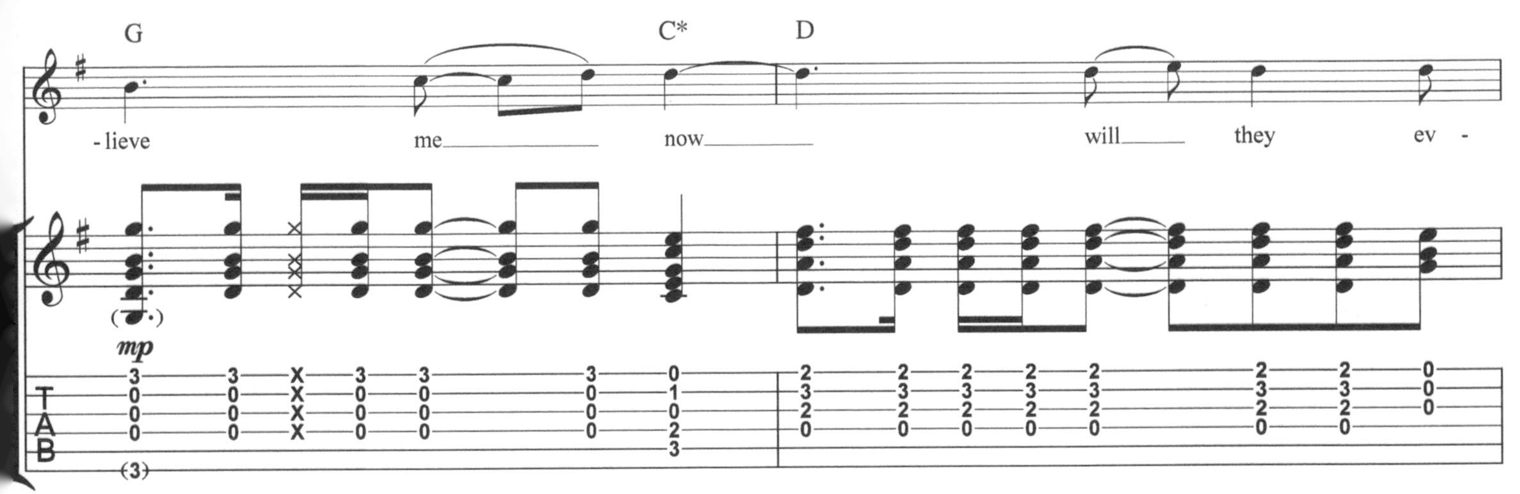
G
C*
D
- lieve me now
will they ev -
mp

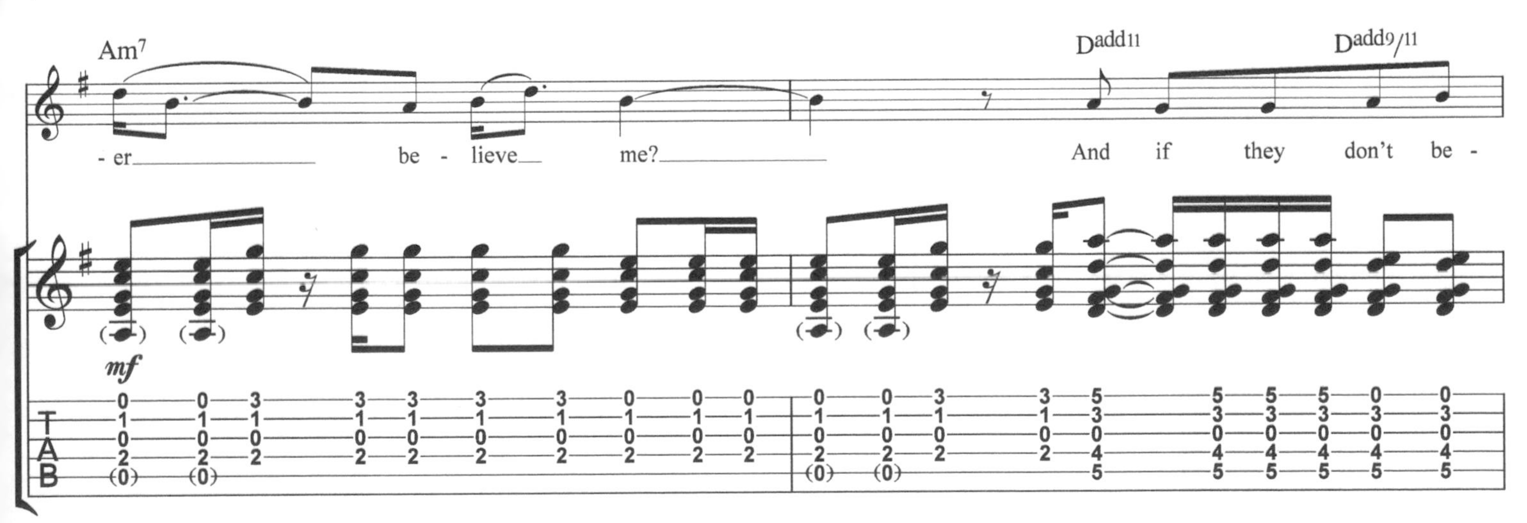
Am7
Dadd11
Dadd9/11
- er be - lieve me?
And if they don't be -
mf

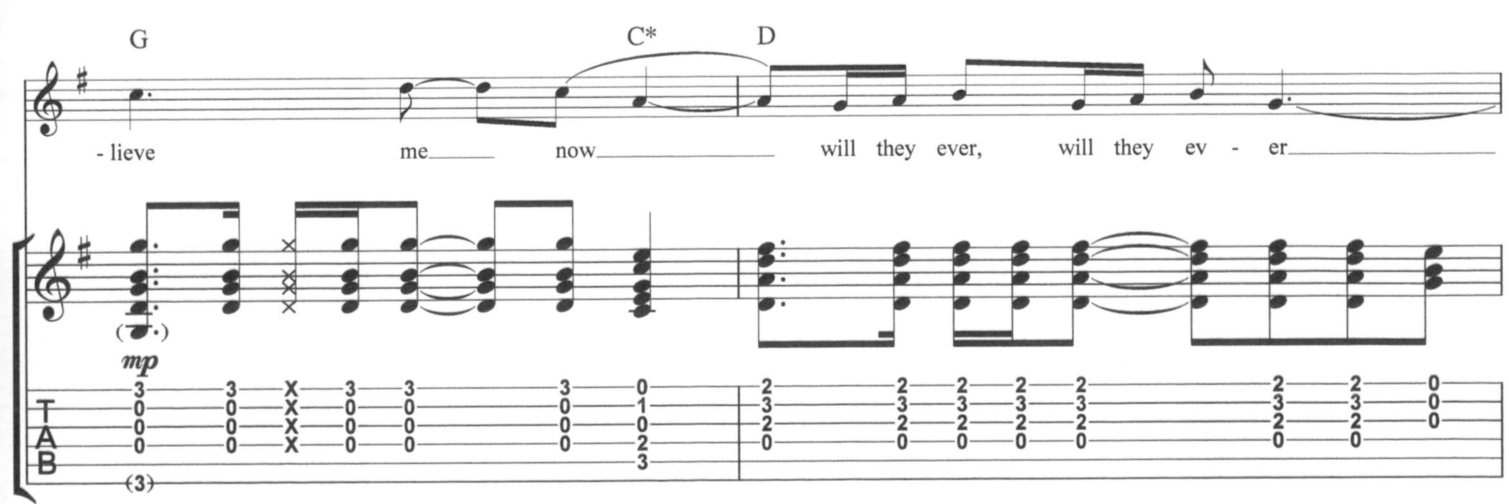
G
C*
D
- lieve me now
will they ever, will they ev - er
mp

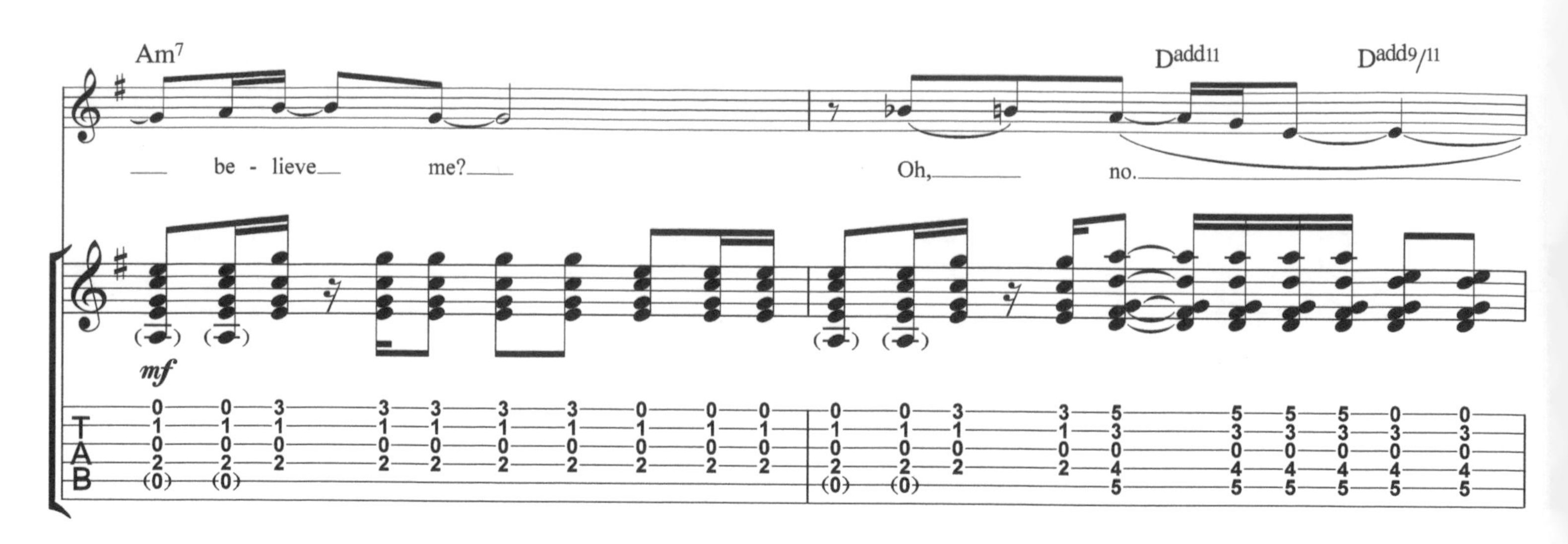
Am7
Dadd11
Dadd9/11
be - lieve me?
Oh,
no.
mf

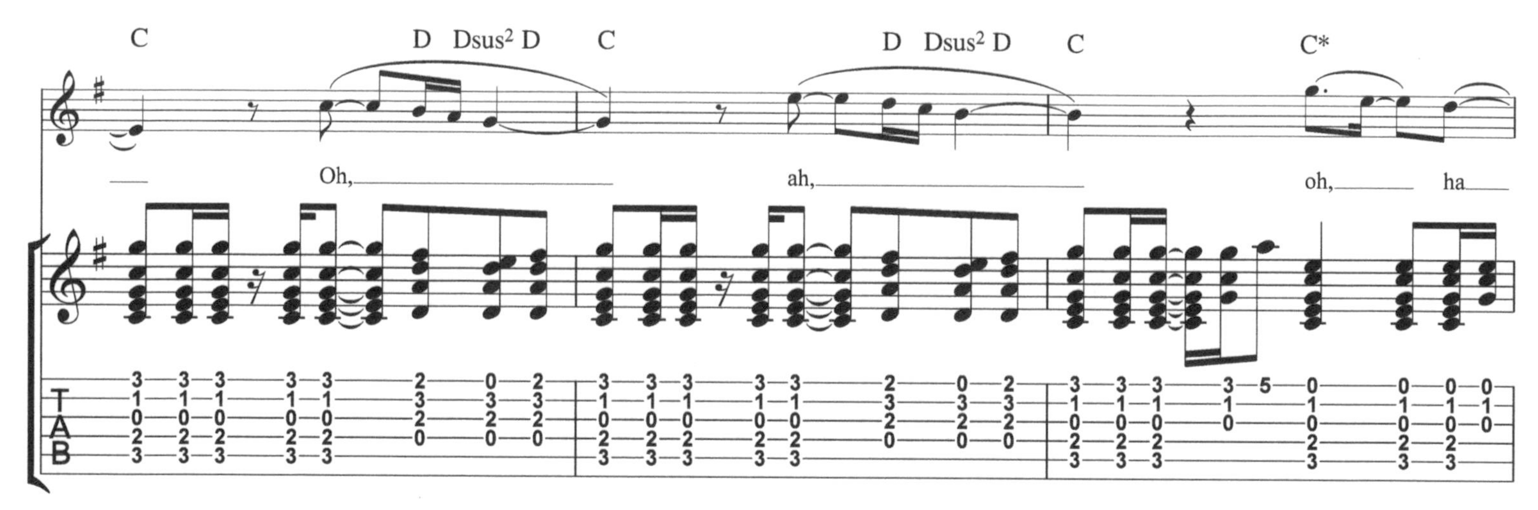
C
D Dsus2 D
C
D Dsus2 D
C
C*
Oh,
ah,
oh,
ha

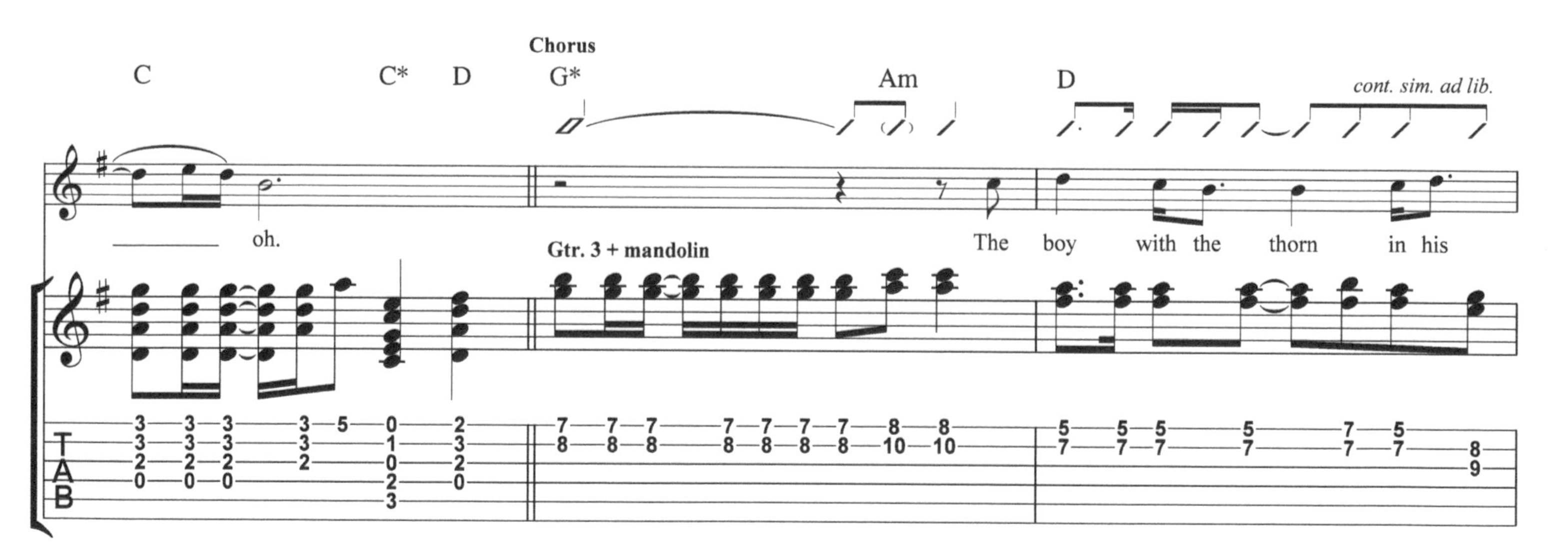
C
C*
D
Chorus
G*
Am
D
cont. sim. ad lib.
oh.
Gtr. 3 + mandolin
The boy with the thorn in his

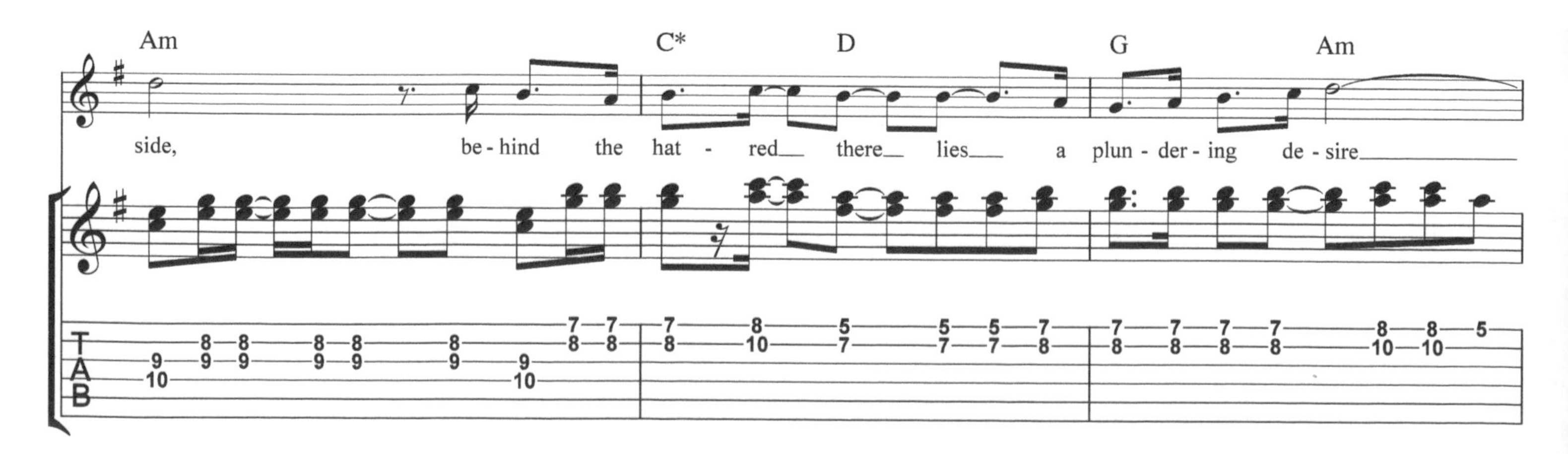
Am
C*
D
G
Am
side,
be - hind the hat - red there lies a plun - der - ing de - sire

D
Am
C*
D
for
love.
2. How can they
Gtrs. 1-3

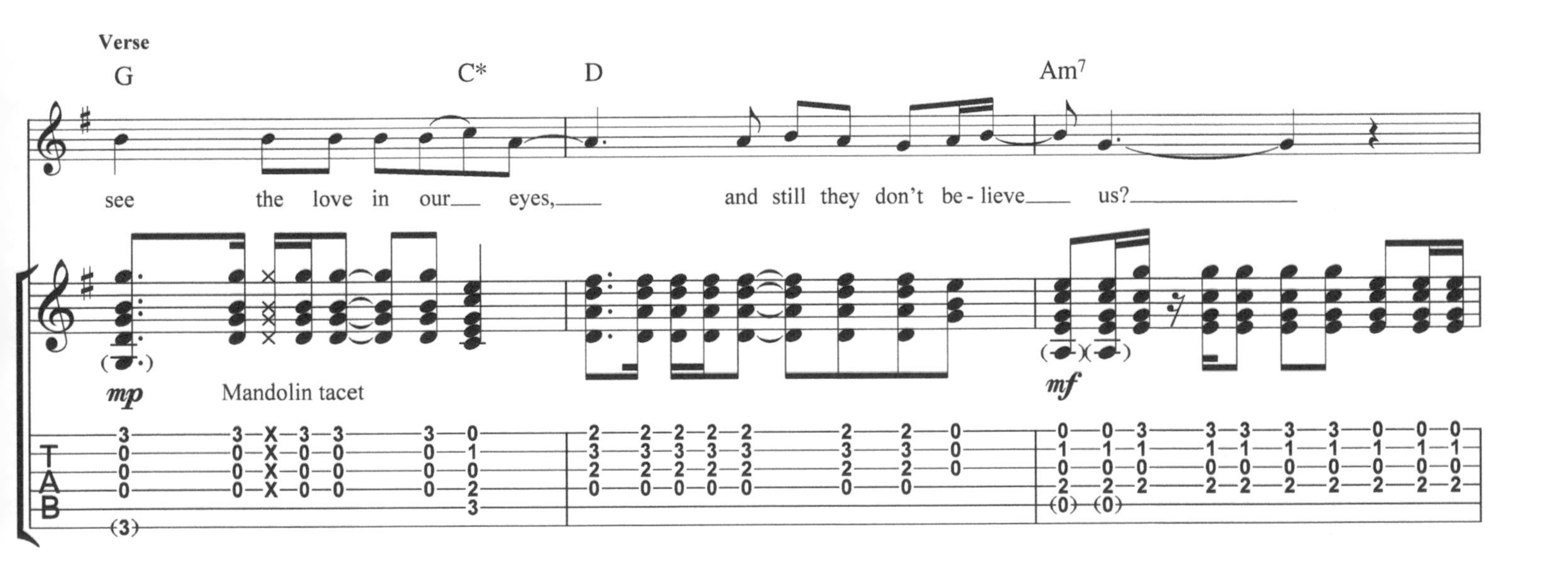
Verse
G
C*
D
Am7
see the love in our eyes, and still they don't be-lieve us?
Mandolin tacet
mp
mf

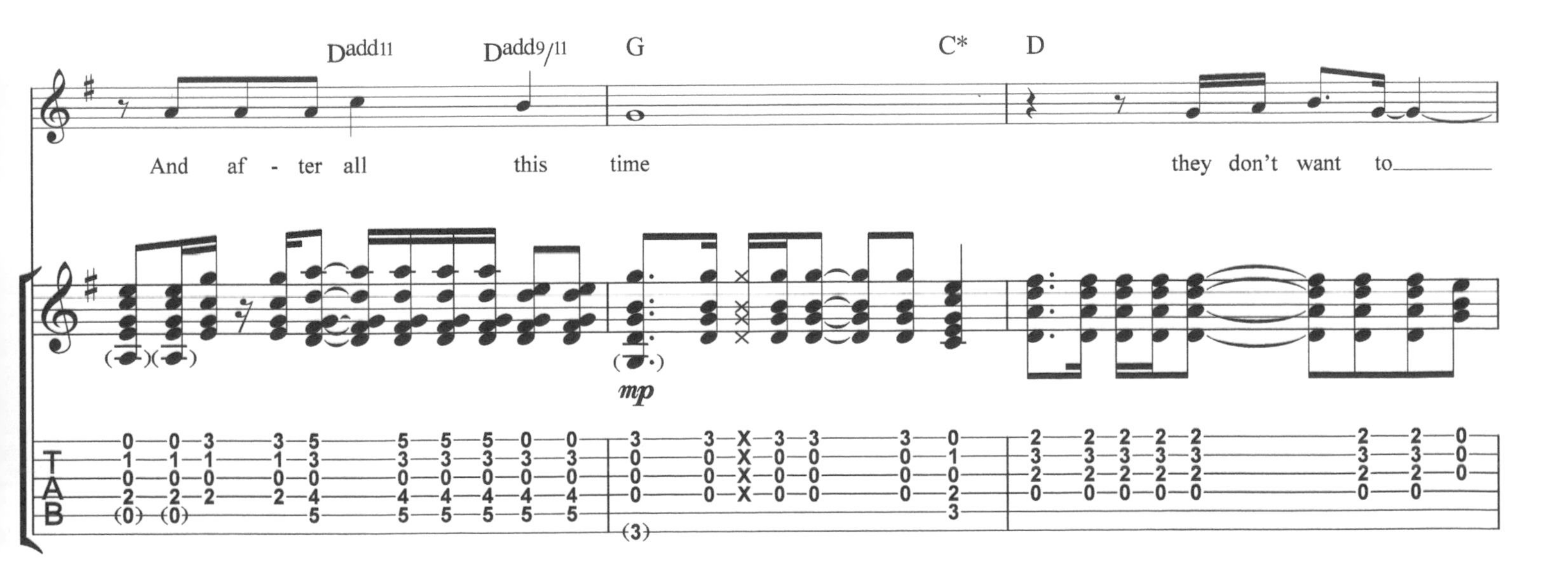
Dadd11
Dadd9/11
G
C*
D
And af - ter all this time they don't want to
mp

Am7
Dadd11
Dadd9/11
G
C*
be - lieve us.
And if they don't be - lieve us now
mf
mp

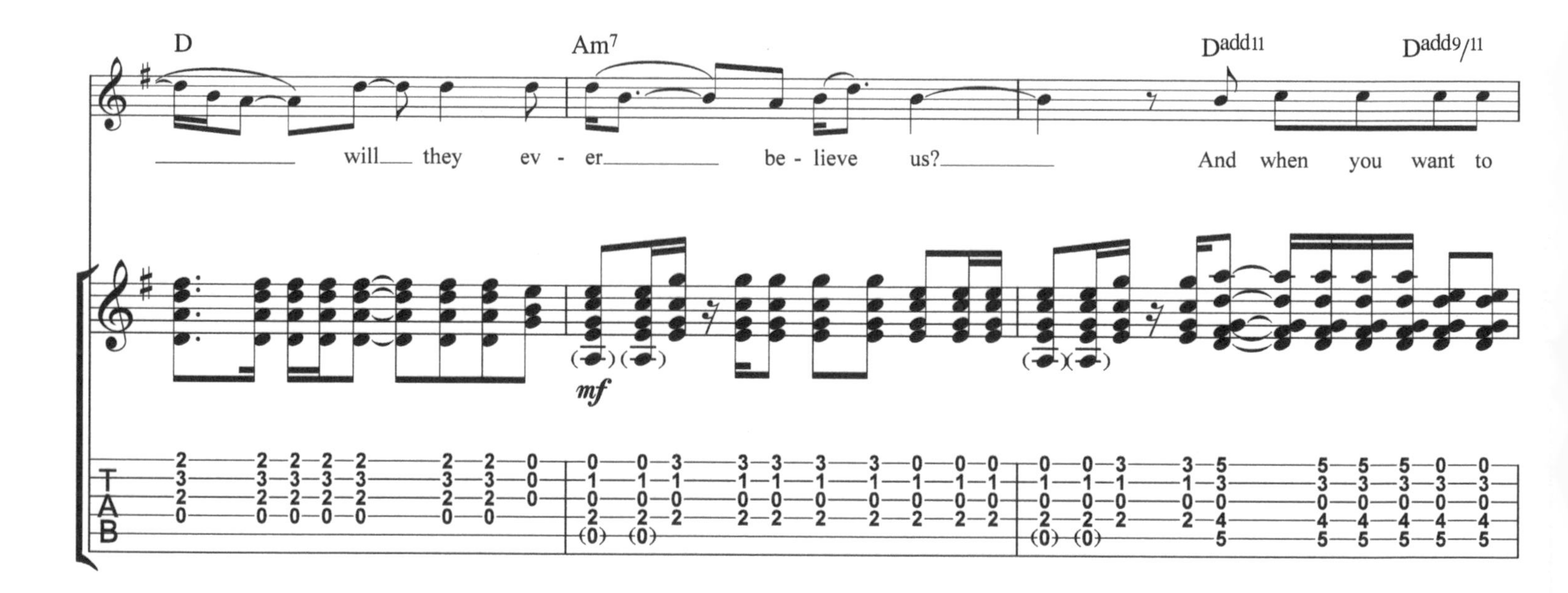
D
Am7
Dadd11
Dadd9/11
will they ev - er be - lieve us?
And when you want to
mf

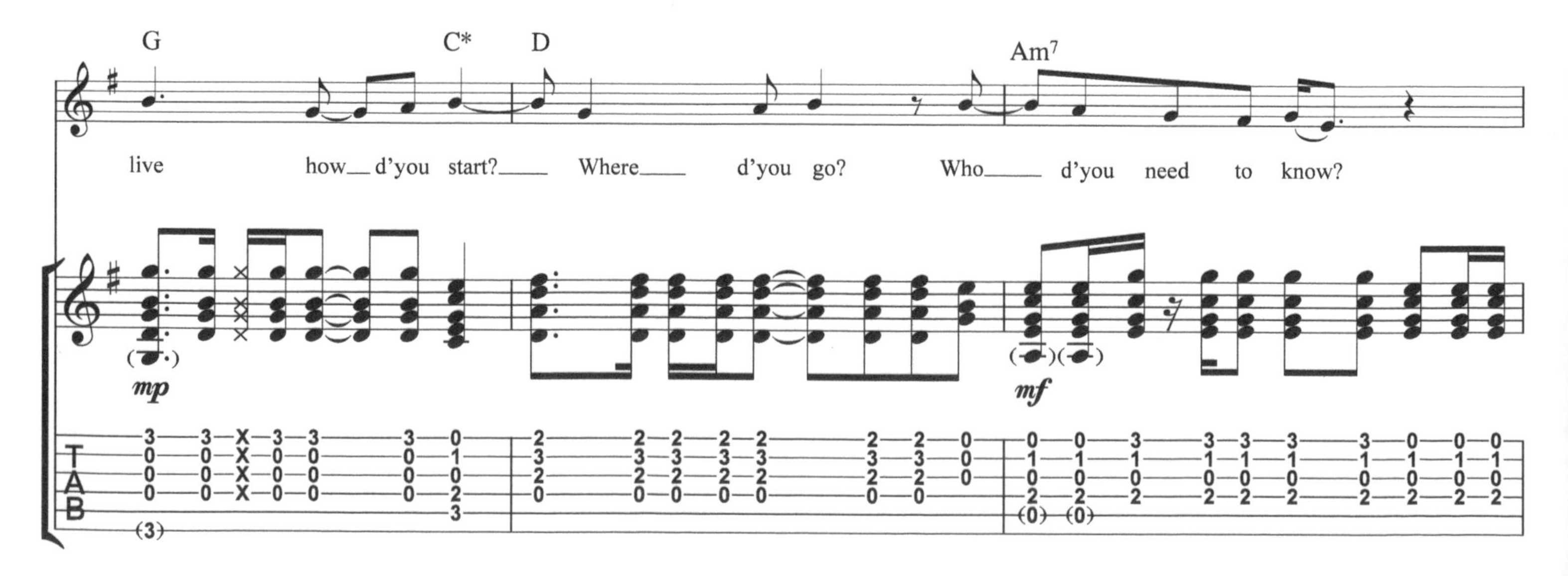
G
C*
D
Am7
live how d'you start? Where d'you go? Who d'you need to know?
mp
mf

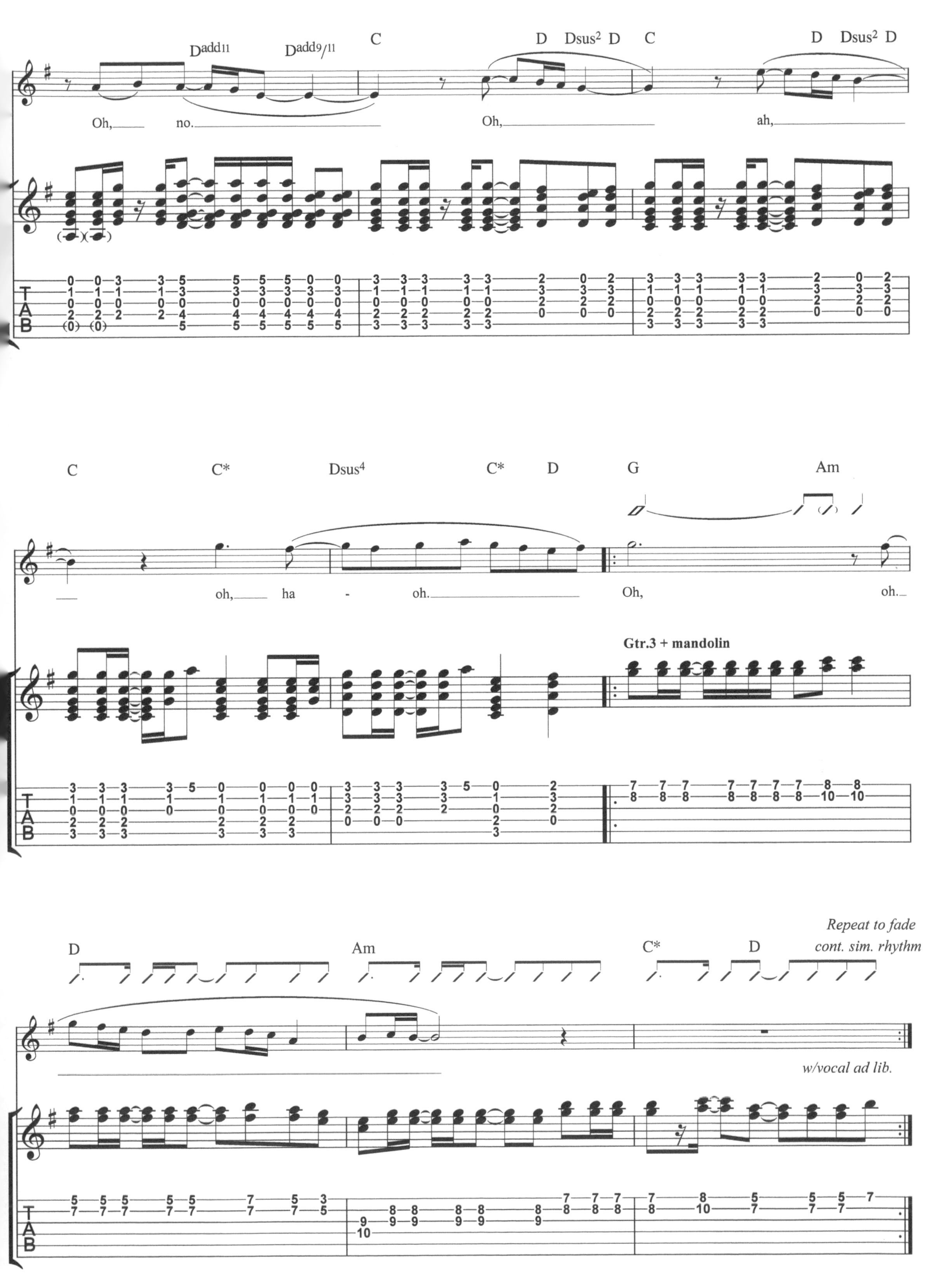
Dadd11
Dadd9/11
C
D Dsus2 D
C
D Dsus2 D
Oh, no.
Oh,
ah,
C
C*
Dsus4
C*
D
G
Am
oh, ha - oh.
Oh,
oh.
Gtr.3 + mandolin
D
Am
C*
D
Repeat to fade
cont. sim. rhythm
w/vocal ad lib.

this charming man

Words & Music by Morrissey & Johnny Marr

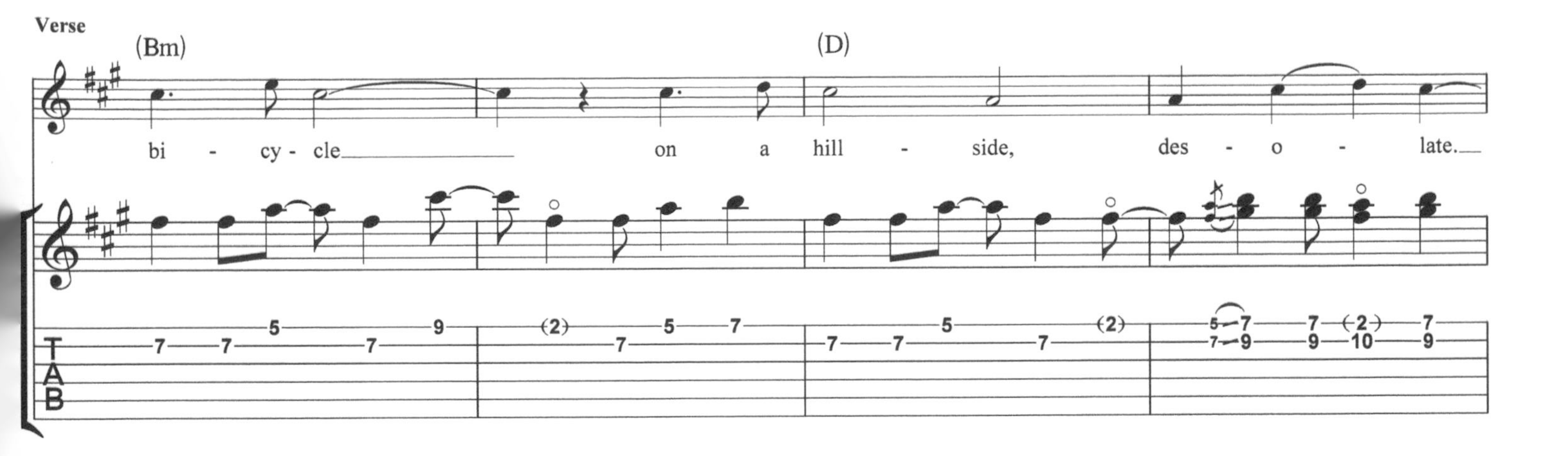
Verse
(Bm)
(D)
bi - cy - cle on a hill - side, des - o - late.

(A)
Will na - ture make a man of me
let ring...
let ring...

(Bm)
(D)
yet? When in this

(A)
charm - ing car this charm - - -
let ring...
let ring...

(Bm)
- ing man.
2. Why

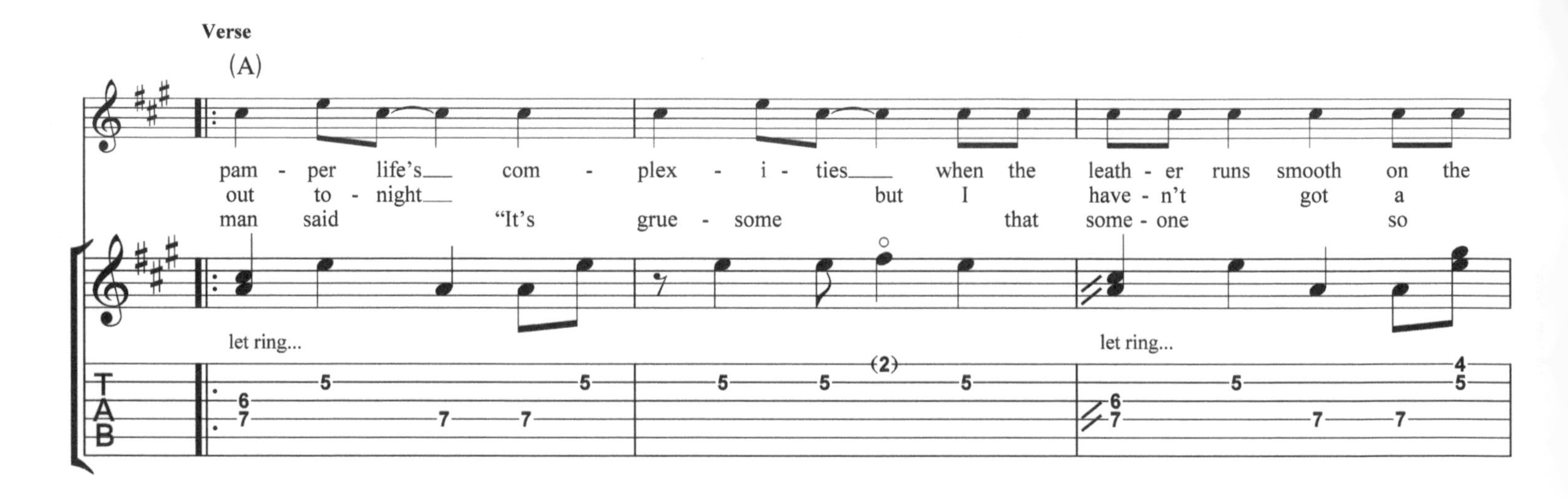
Verse
(A)
pam - per life's com - plex - i - ties when the leath - er runs smooth on the
out to - night but I have - n't got a
man said "It's grue - some that some - one so
let ring...
let ring...

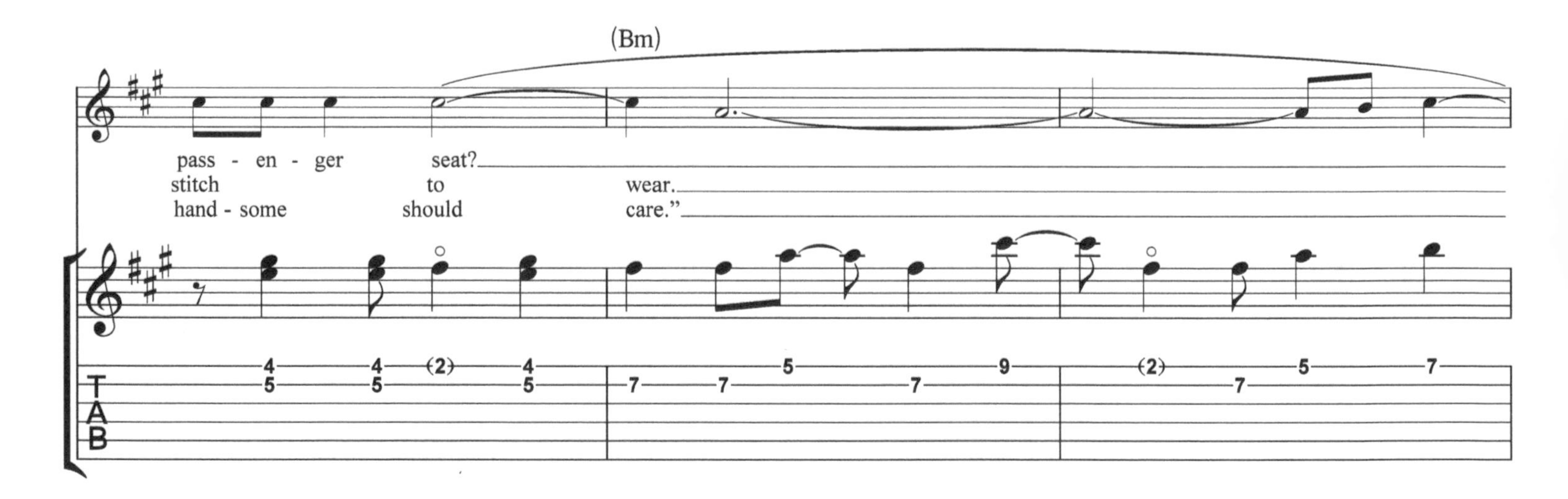
(Bm)
pass - en - ger seat?
stitch to wear.
hand - some should care."

(D)
1, 2.
3.
Chorus
(D)
I would go
This
Ah!
A
let ring...

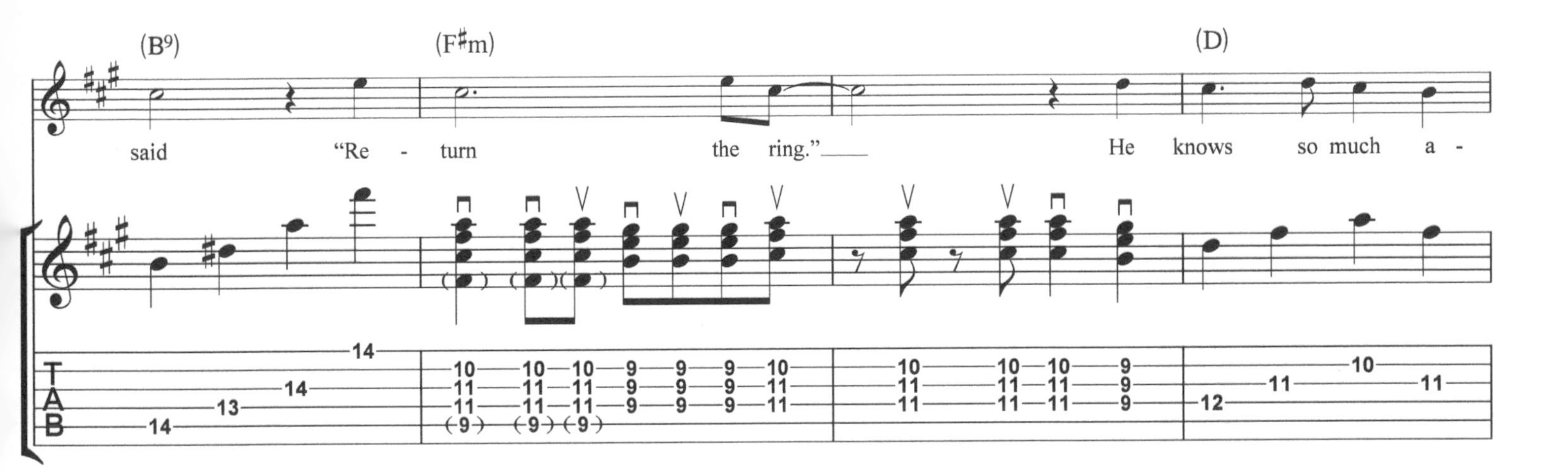

To Coda ⊕

(E6) (F#m) (B9) (D) (B7)

bout these things. He knows so much a - bout these

TAB

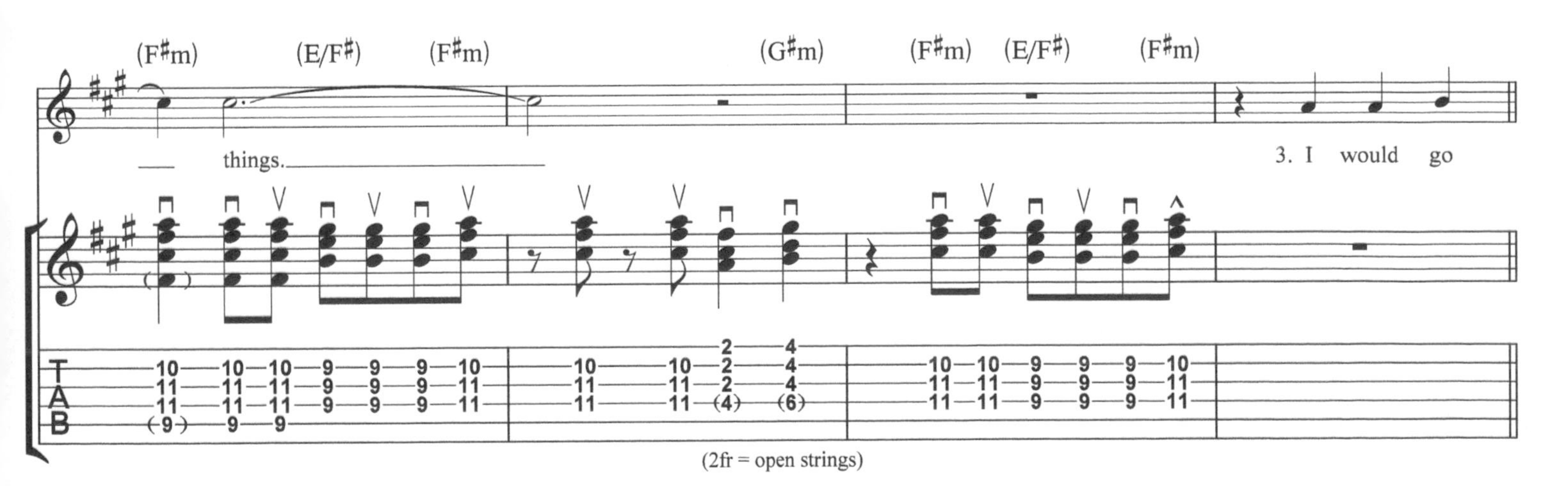

Verse

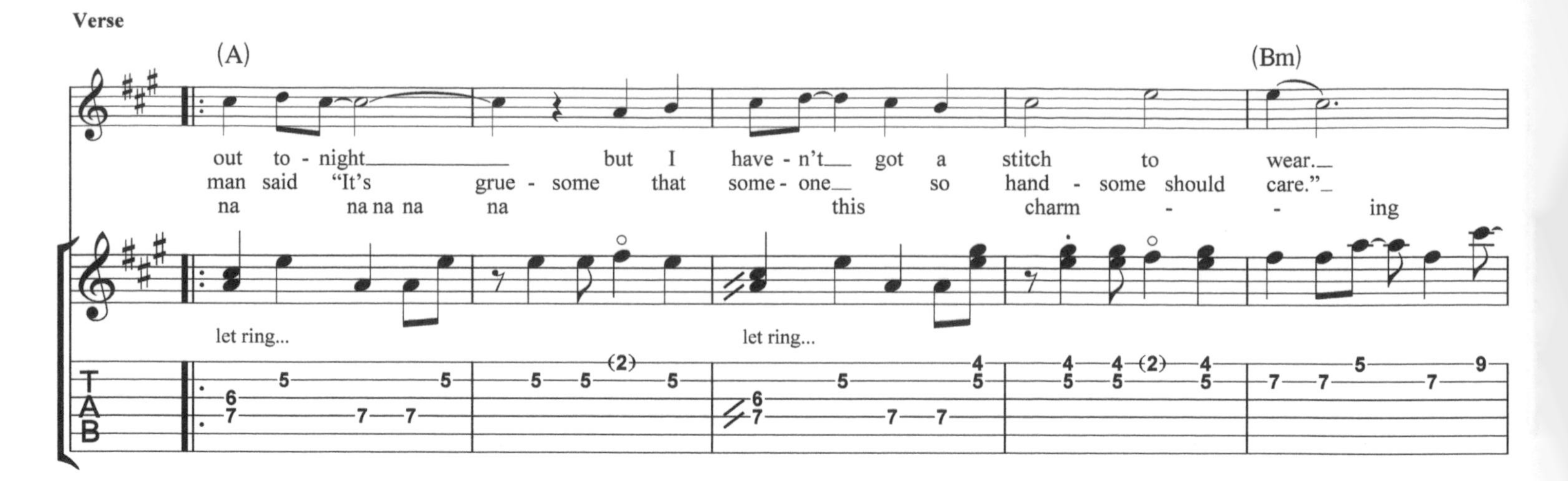
(A)
(Bm)
out to - night but I have - n't got a stitch to wear.
man said "It's grue - some that some - one so hand - some should care."
na na na na na this charm - - ing
let ring...
let ring...

(D)
1-3.
4.
D.S. al Coda
2° This
3° & 4° Na na
Ah!
man.

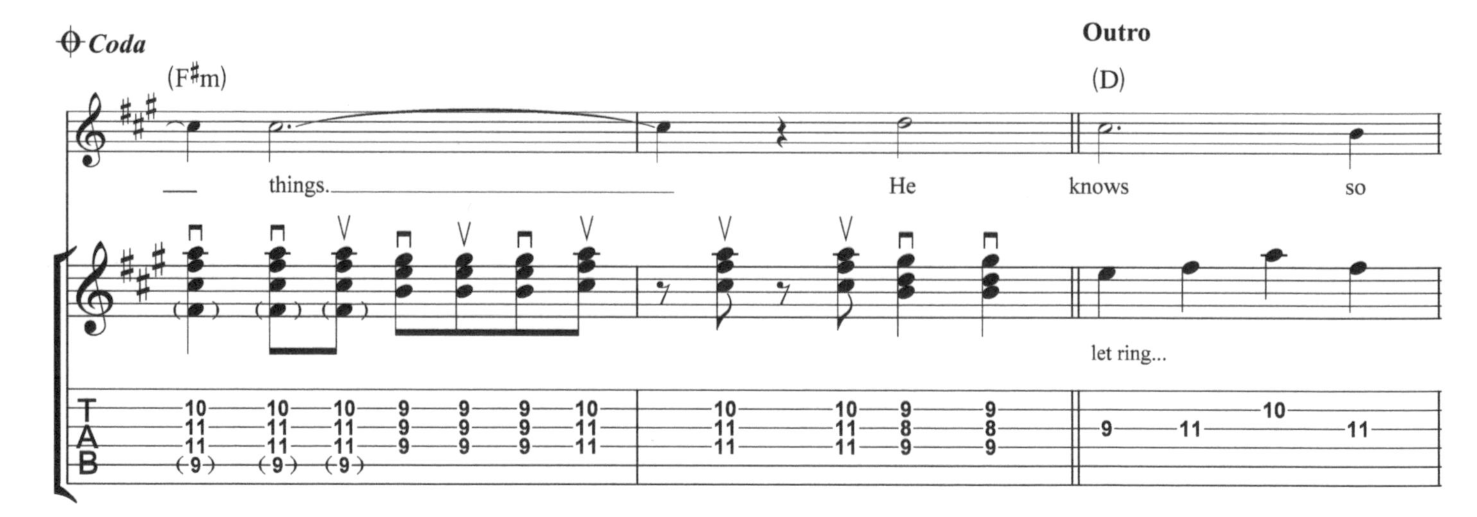
Coda
(F#m)
Outro
(D)
things. He knows so
let ring...

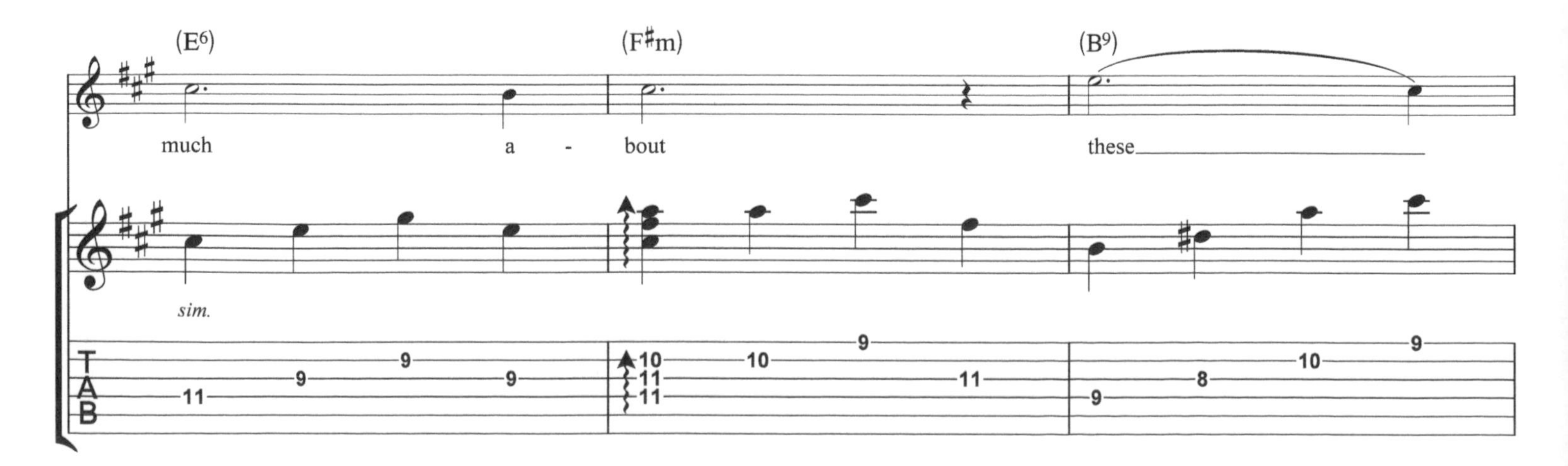
(E6)
(F#m)
(B9)
much a - bout these
sim.

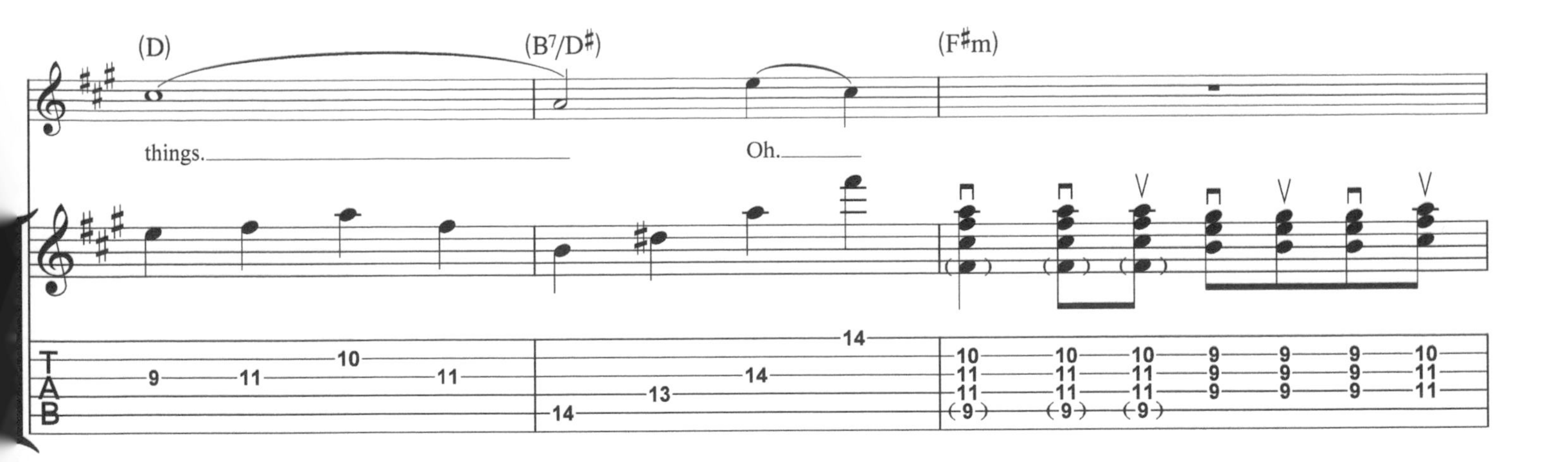
(D)
(B7/D♯)
(F♯m)
things.
Oh.
TAB

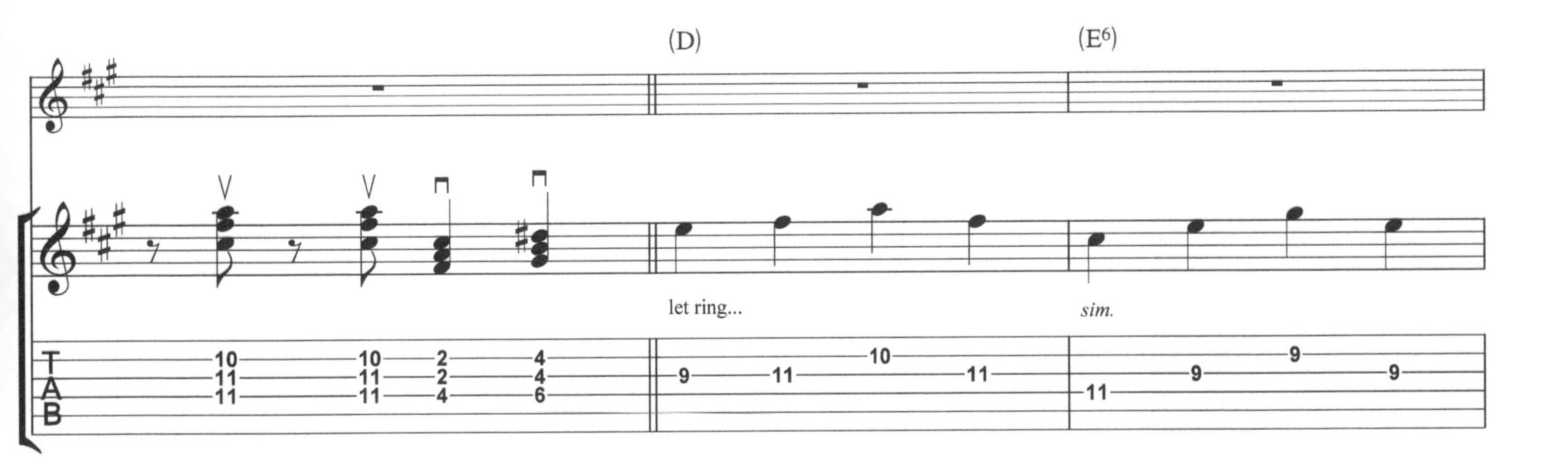
(D)
(E6)
let ring...
sim.
TAB

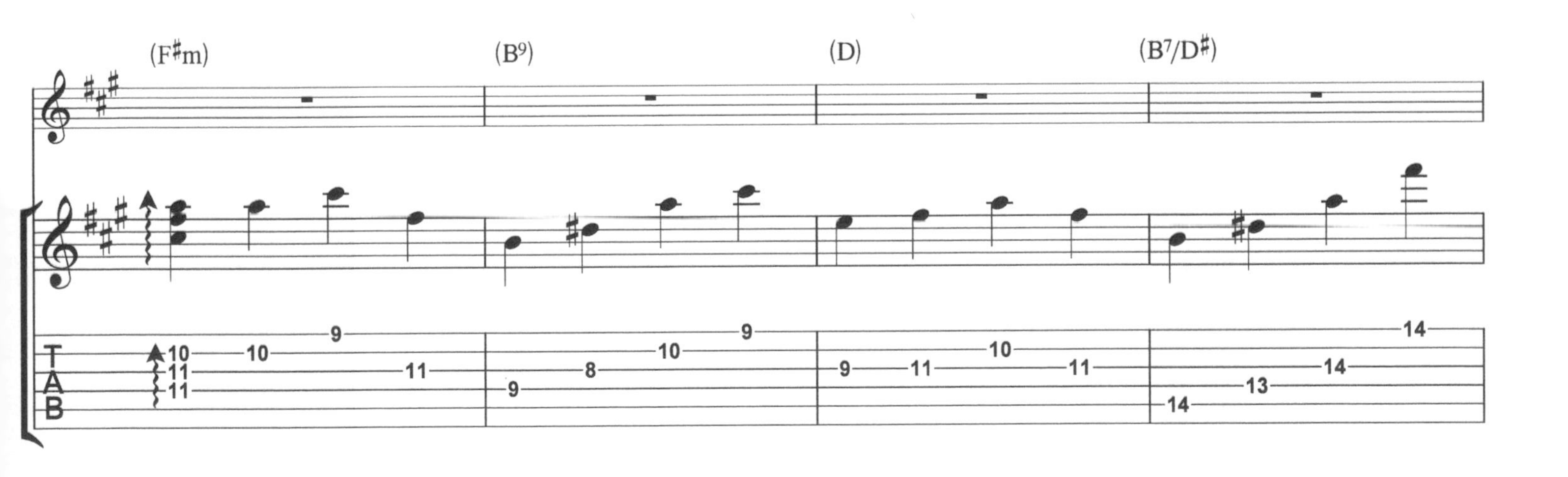
(F♯m)
(B9)
(D)
(B7/D♯)
TAB

(F♯m)
TAB

what difference does it make?

Words & Music by Morrissey & Johnny Marr

Gtr. 2 (no capo)

B5 E5 F♯ A5 D5

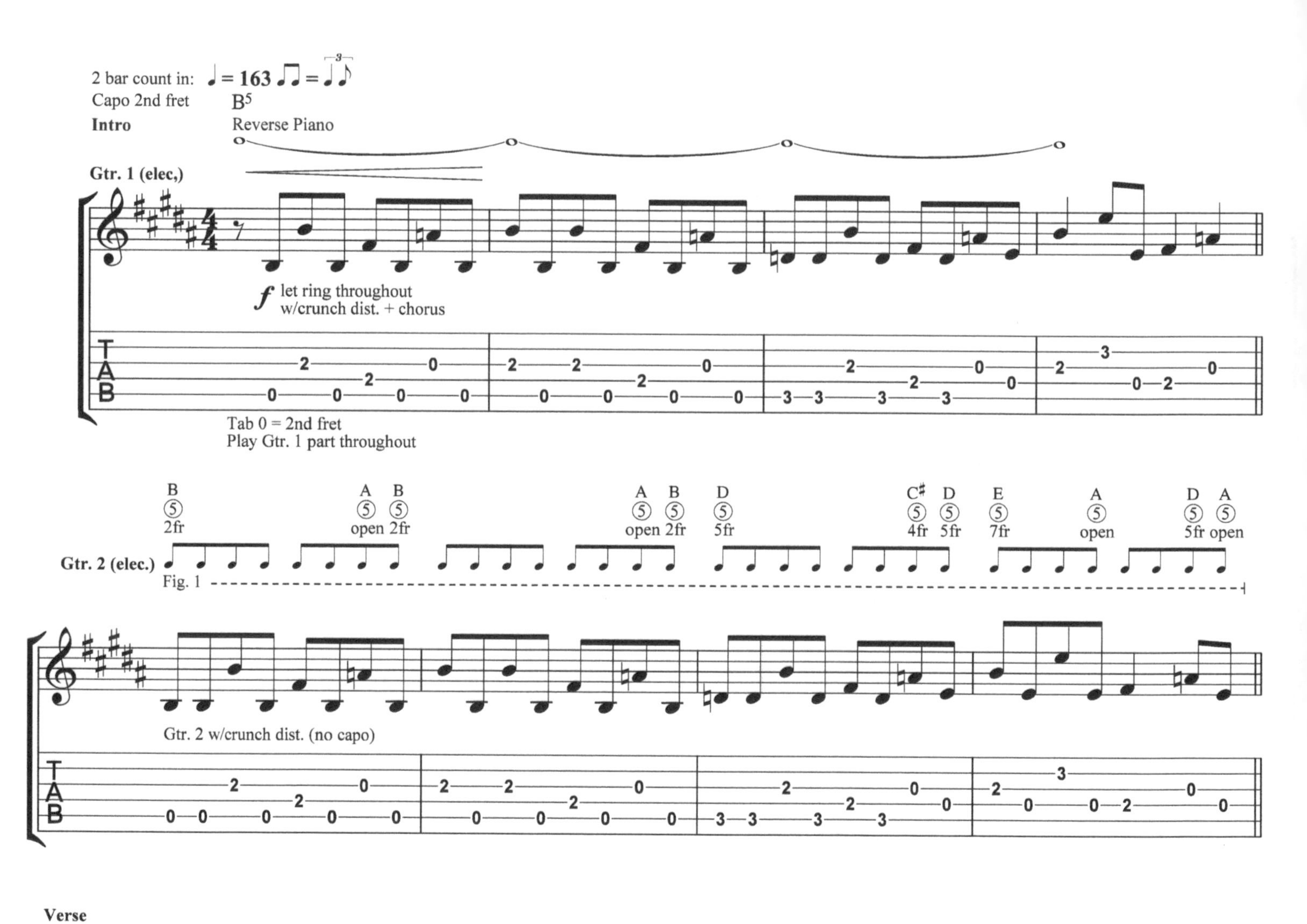

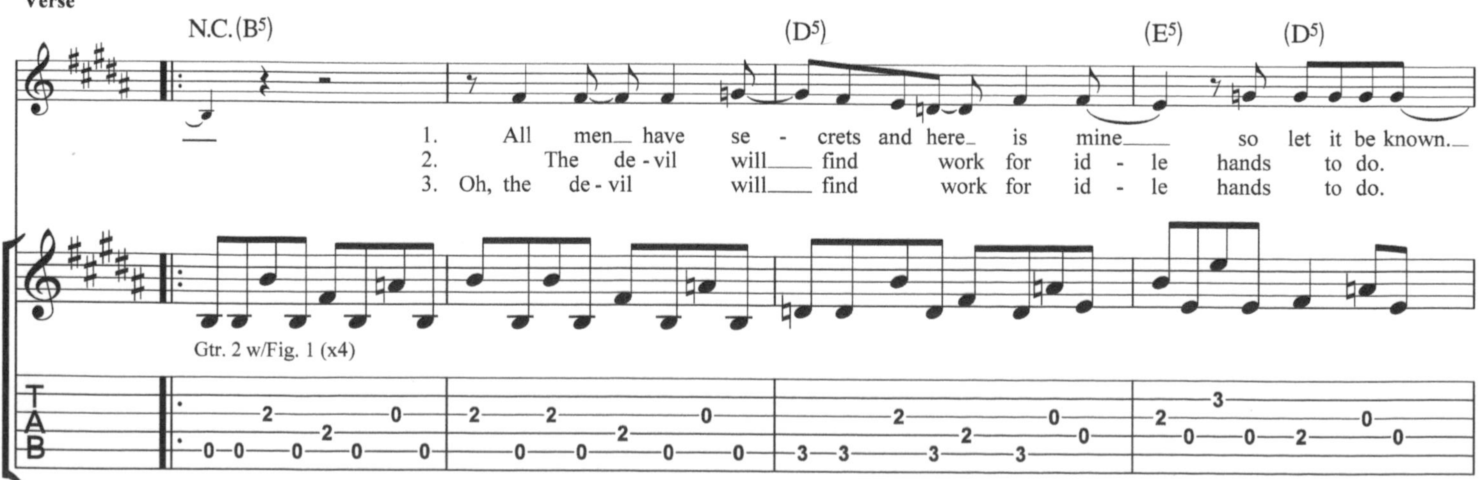

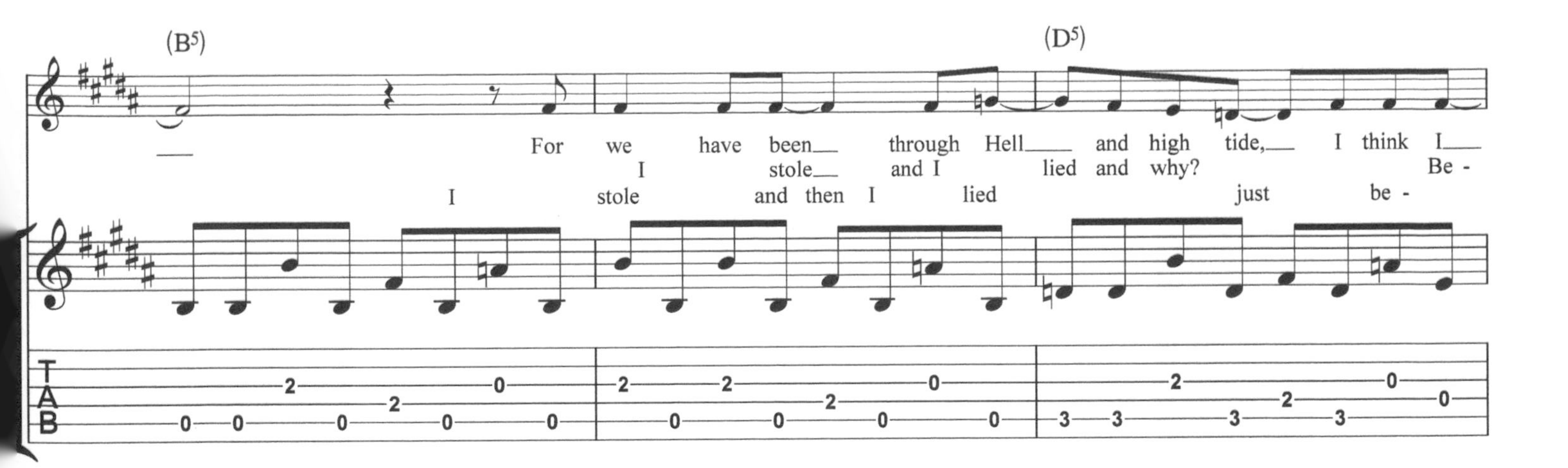
(B5)
(D5)
For we have been through Hell and high tide, I think I
I stole and I lied and why? Be -
I stole and then I lied just be -
T
A
B

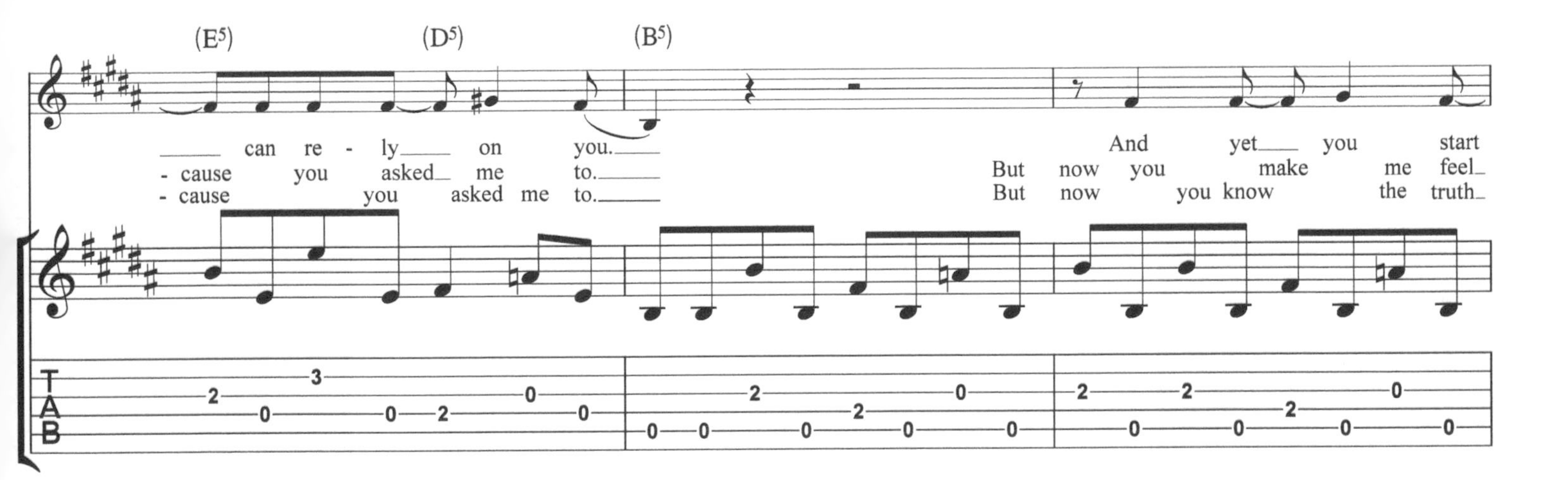
(E5)
(D5)
(B5)
can re - ly on you. And yet you start
- cause you asked me to. But now you make me feel
- cause you asked me to. But now you know the truth
T
A
B

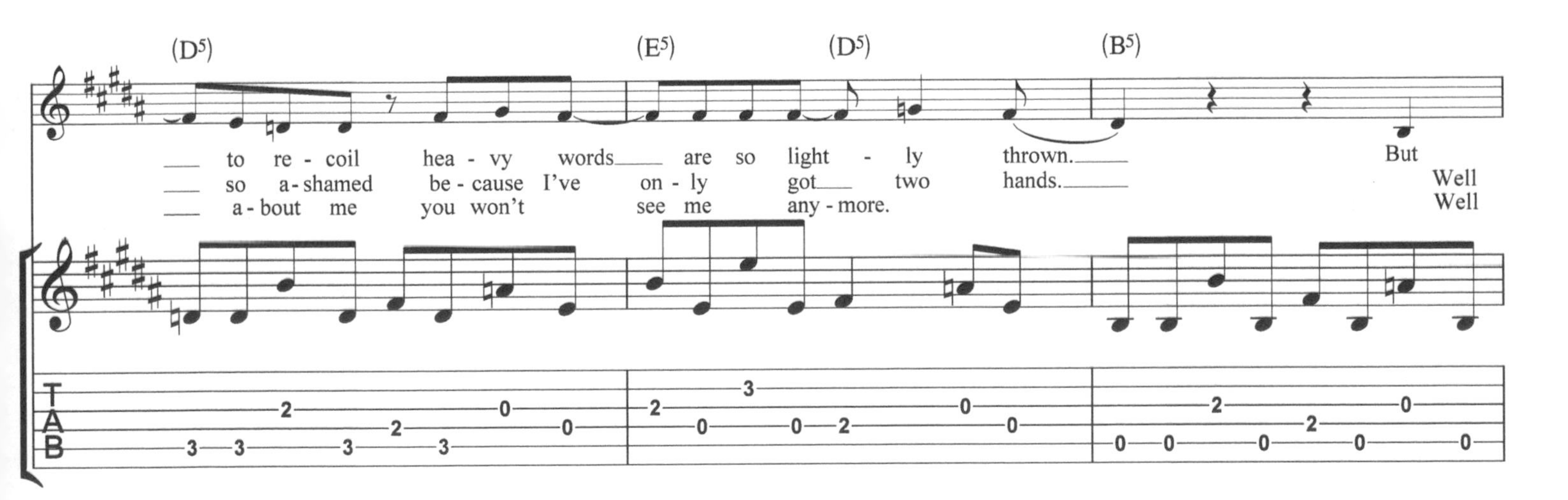
(D5)
(E5)
(D5)
(B5)
to re - coil hea - vy words are so light - ly thrown. But
so a - shamed be - cause I've on - ly got two hands. Well
a - bout me you won't see me any - more. Well
T
A
B

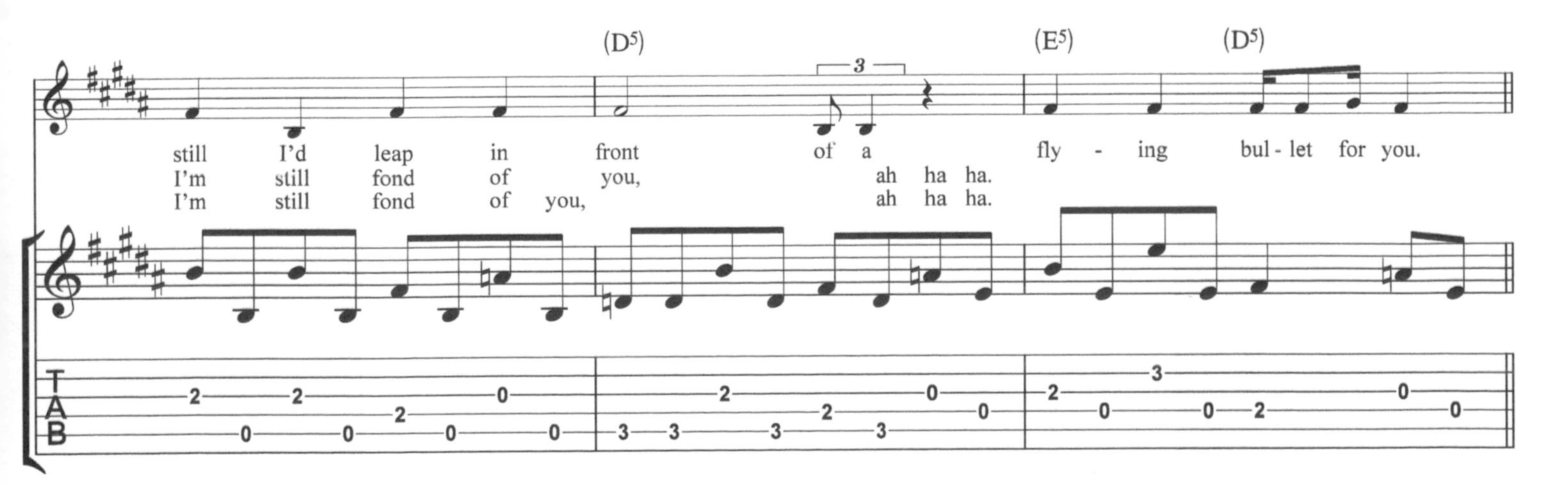
(D5)
(E5)
(D5)
3
still I'd leap in front of a fly - ing bul - let for you.
I'm still fond of you, ah ha ha.
I'm still fond of you, ah ha ha.
T
A
B

Chorus
Gtr. 2
B5
E5
F#5
A5
1. 2. So what diff - erence does it make?
3. But no more a - po - lo - gies, no more,
let ring...
sim.

B5
E5
F#5
A5
So what diff - erence does it make?
no more a - po - po - gies, oh.

G# ⑥ 4fr
G# ④ 6fr
D# ⑤ 6fr
C# ⑤ 4fr
E ④ 2fr
F# ⑥ 2fr
G ⑥ 3fr
1. It makes none but now you have gone and you
2. It makes none but now you have gone and your
3. I'm too tired, I'm so sick and tired and I'm

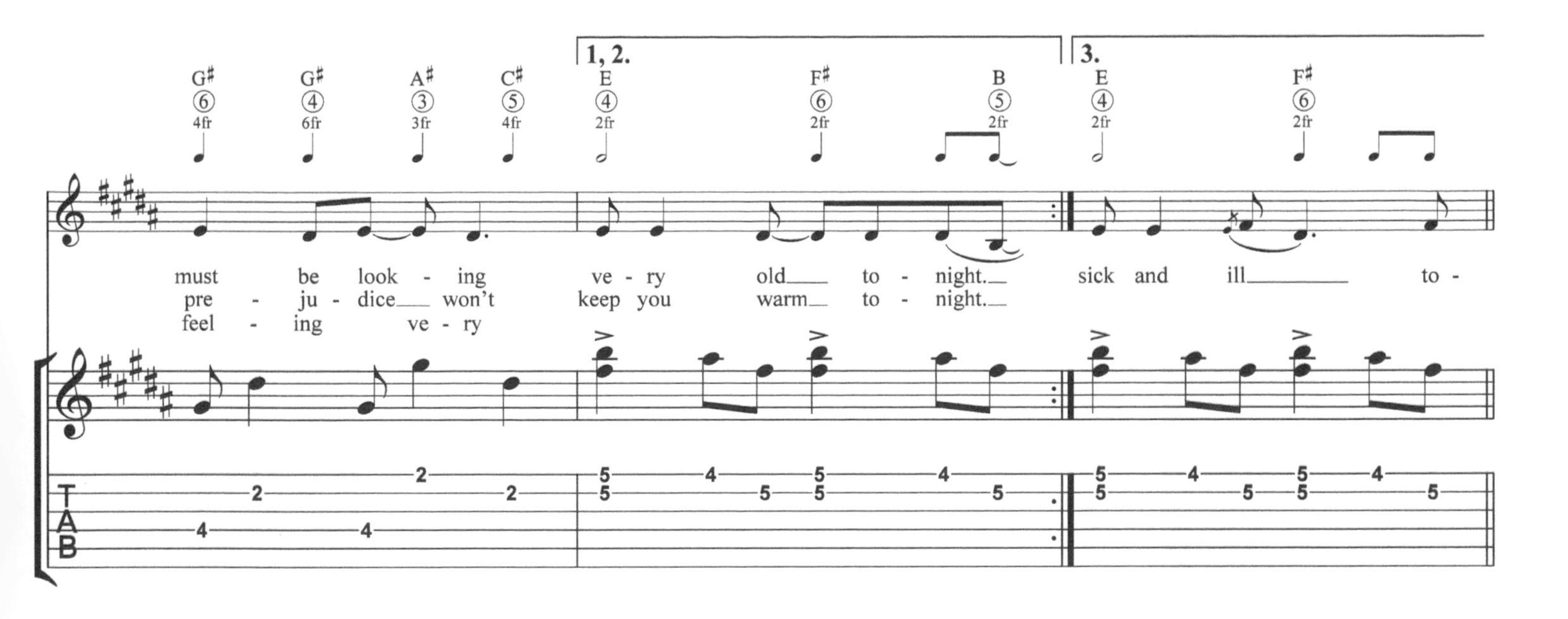
1, 2.
3.
G♯ G♯ A♯ C♯ E F♯ B E F♯
must be look - ing ve - ry old to - night. sick and ill to -
pre - ju - dice won't keep you warm to - night.
feel - ing ve - ry

B5 D5 E5 D5
day. But I'm still fond of you, ah ha ha.
Fig. 2

B5 D5 E5 D5
Gtr. 1 w/Fig.2

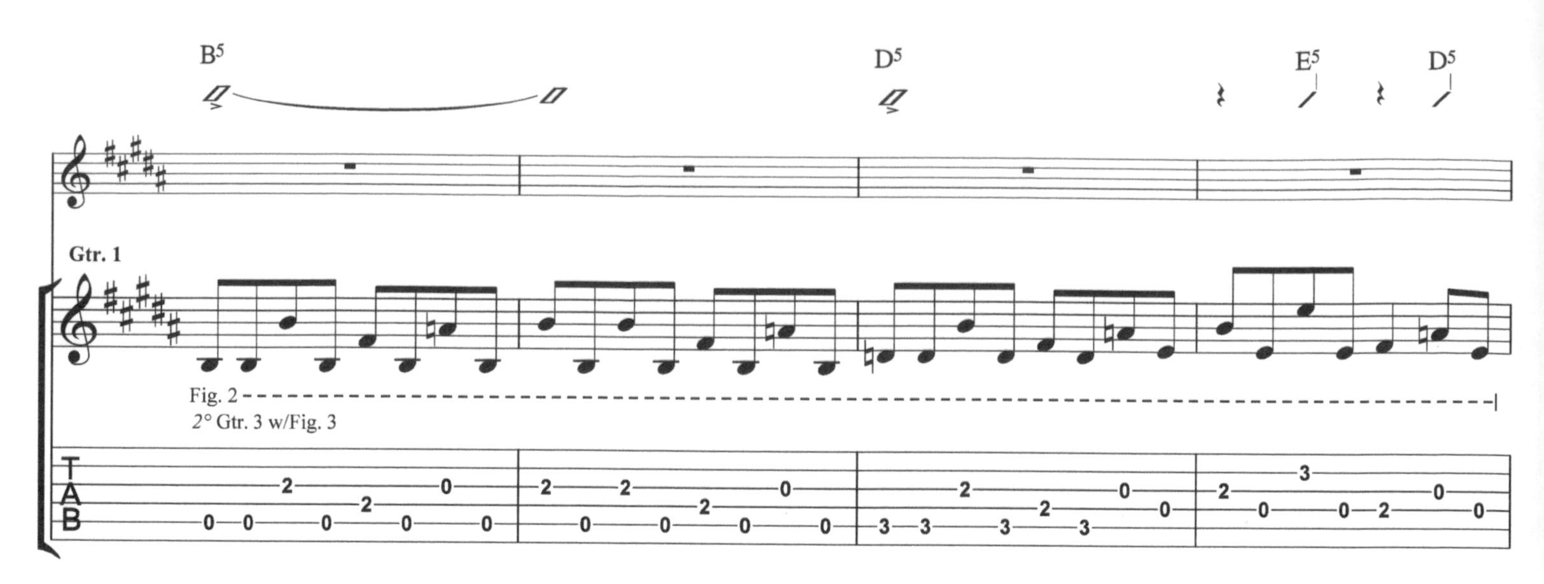
B5
D5
E5
D5
Gtr. 1
Fig. 2
2° Gtr. 3 w/Fig. 3
TAB

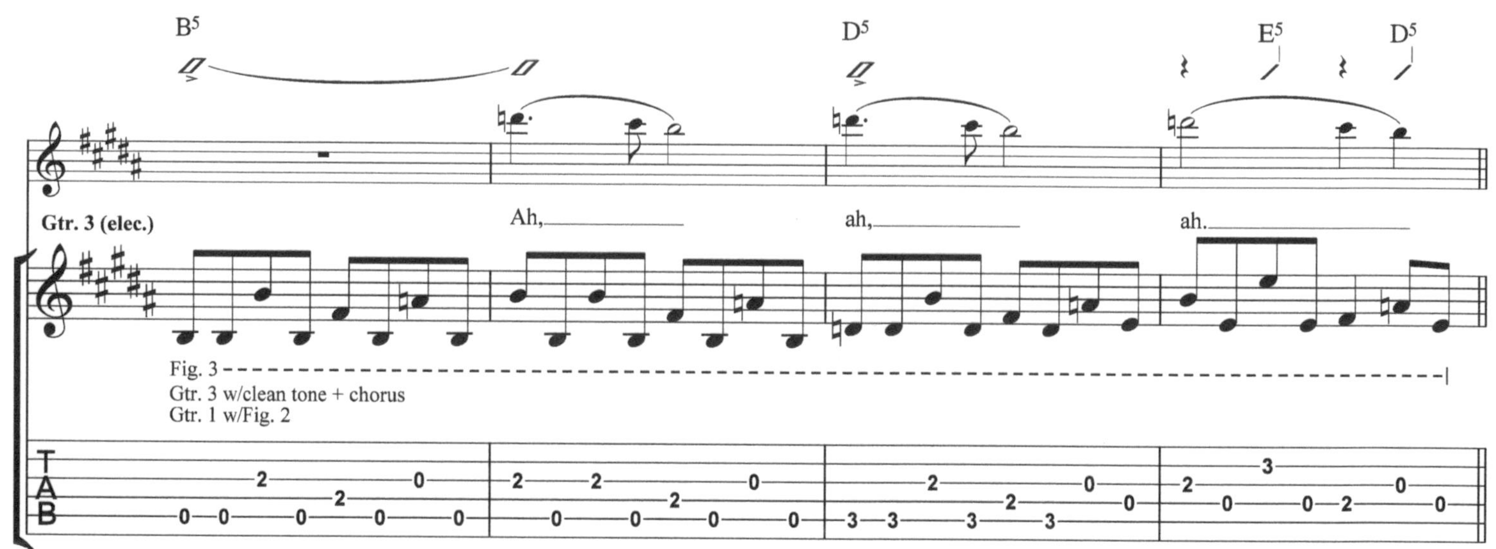
B5
D5
E5
D5
Gtr. 3 (elec.)
Ah,
ah,
ah.
Fig. 3
Gtr. 3 w/clean tone + chorus
Gtr. 1 w/Fig. 2
TAB

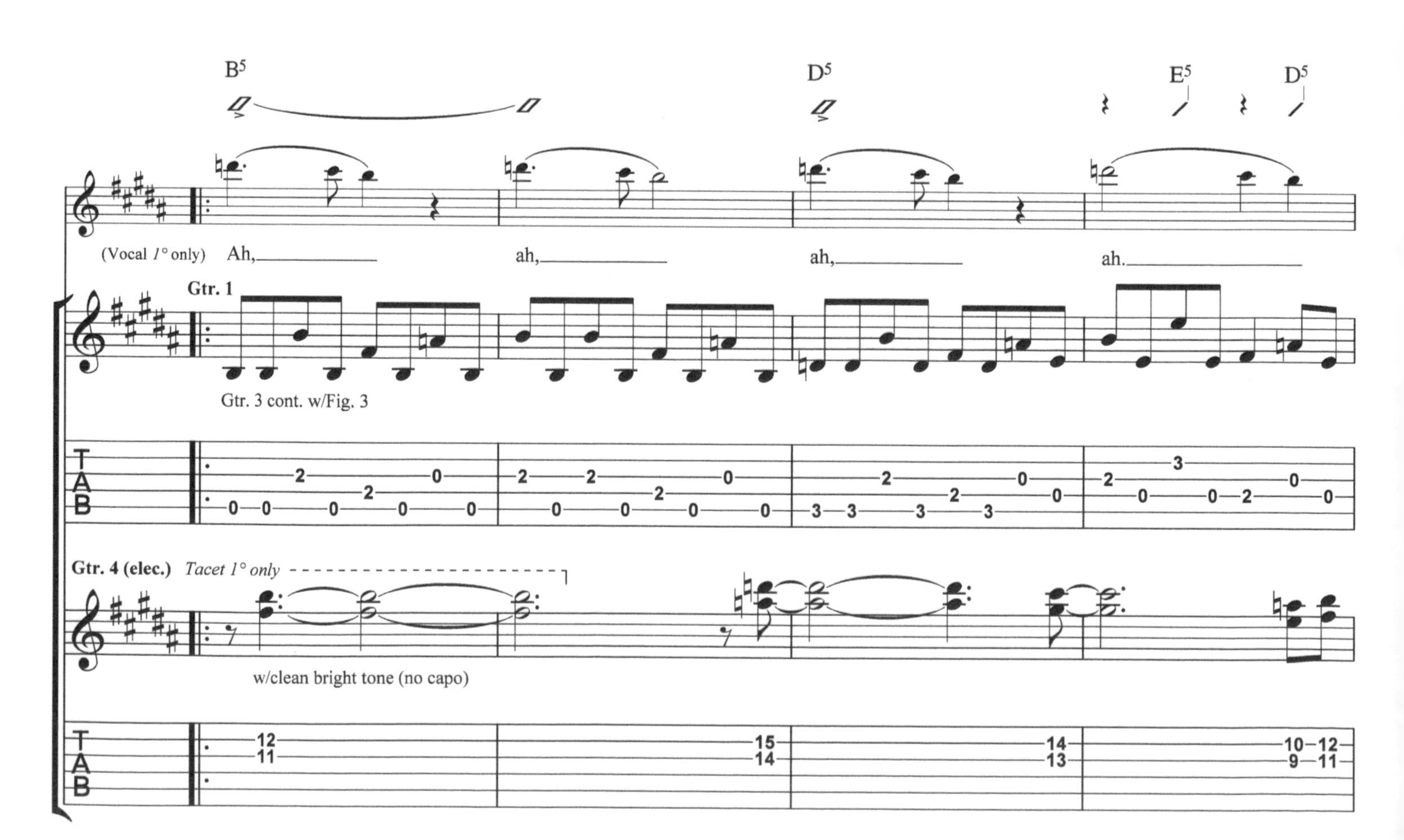
B5
D5
E5
D5
(Vocal 1° only)
Ah,
ah,
ah,
ah.
Gtr. 1
Gtr. 3 cont. w/Fig. 3
TAB
Gtr. 4 (elec.)
Tacet 1° only
w/clean bright tone (no capo)
TAB

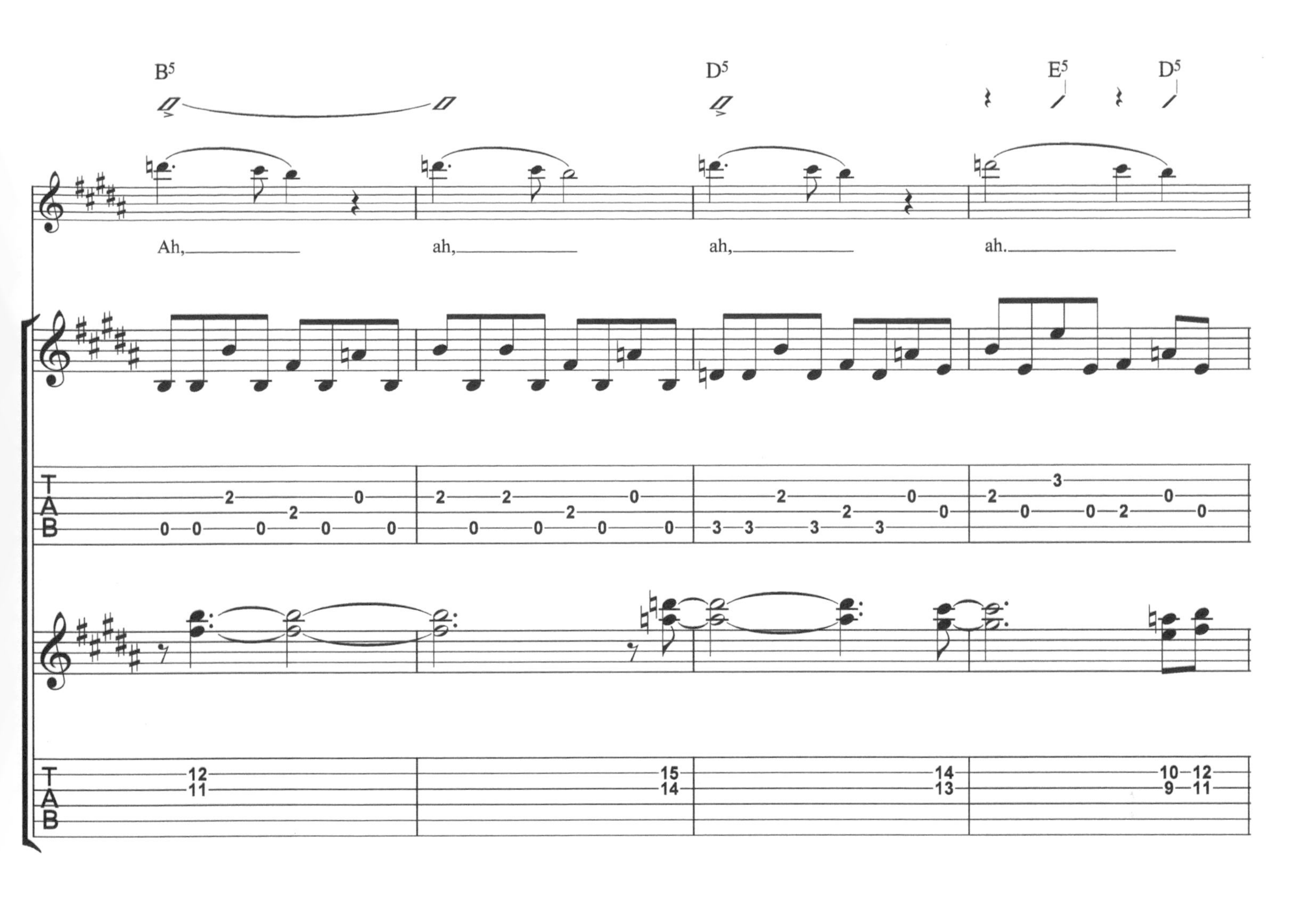
B5
D5
E5
D5
Ah,
ah,
ah,
ah.

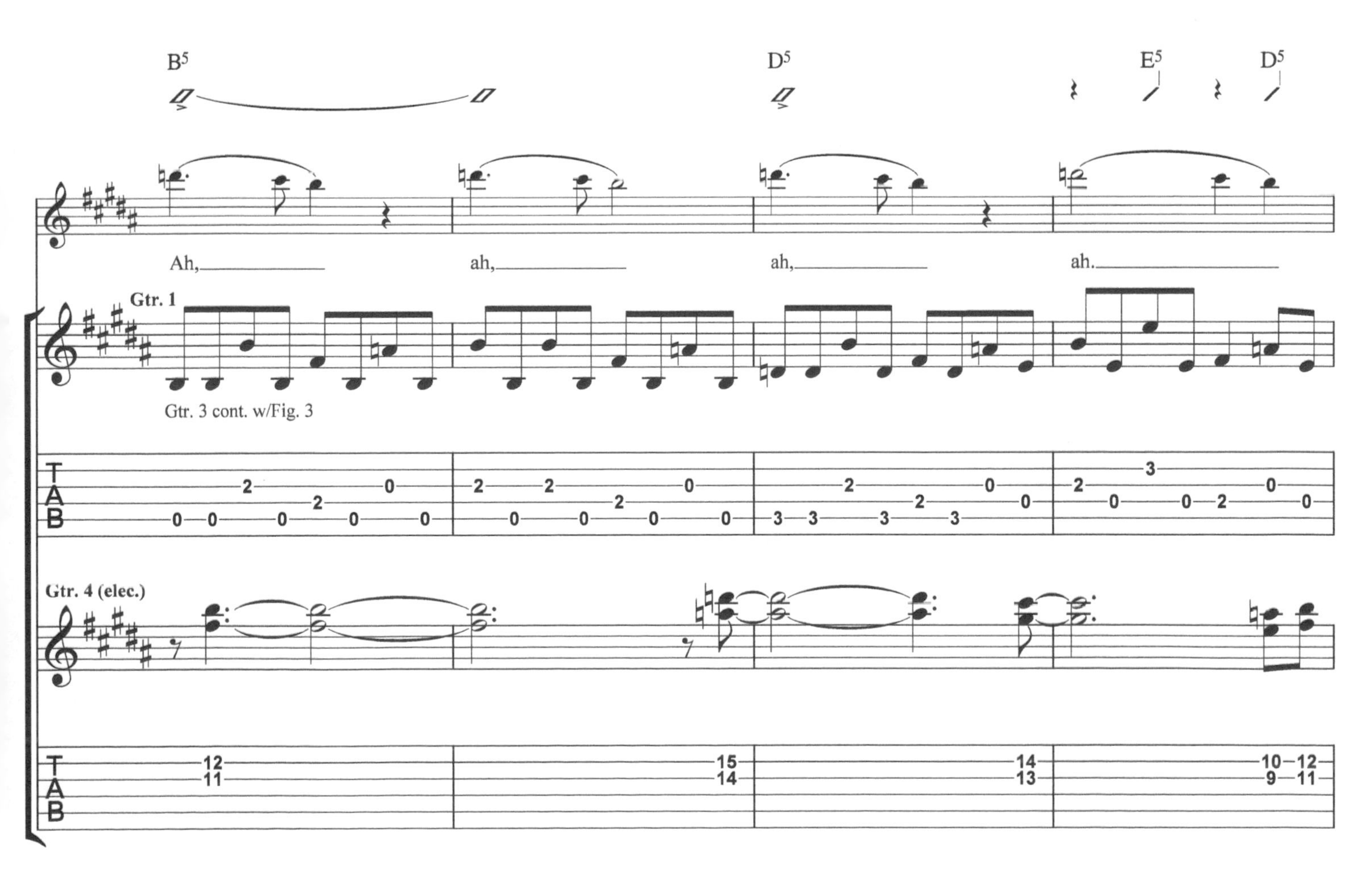
B5
D5
E5
D5
Ah,
ah,
ah,
ah.
Gtr. 1
Gtr. 3 cont. w/Fig. 3
Gtr. 4 (elec.)

B5
D5
E5
D5
Ah.
T
A
B
B5
D5
E5
D5
B5
B5

Online Audio Track Listing

1 tuning notes

Full instrumental performances (with guitar)...

2 bigmouth strikes again

3 heaven knows I'm miserable now

4 panic

5 the boy with the thorn in his side

6 this charming man

7 what difference does it make?

Backing tracks only (without guitar)...

8 bigmouth strikes again

9 heaven knows I'm miserable now

10 panic

11 the boy with the thorn in his side

12 this charming man

13 what difference does it make?

all tracks: